THE ROAD TO BURNS:
FINAL STANDDOWN
AT THE
OREGON STANDOFF

True Crime Defense Attorney Case Files: Book 2

by

MIKE ARNOLD
&
EMILIA GARDNER

Versus
Publishing
Eugene, Ore.

Published by:
Versus Publishing
401 East 10th Ave, Suite 400, Eugene, Oregon 97401
Phone: (541) 525-9117
www.facebook.com/versuspublishing
twitter.com/versusbooks
www.versuspublishing.com

Title: The Road to Burns: Final Standdown at the Oregon
Standoff

ISBN: 978-0-9978484-7-2
Authors: Mike Arnold and Emilia Gardner

Disclaimer: This book is a work of creative nonfiction, which Lee
Gutkind, the godfather of the genre, defines as "nonfiction that
employs techniques like scene, dialogue, description, while
allowing personal point of view and voice (reflection) rather than
maintaining the sham of objectivity." The authors do not claim to
be objective, and whenever we determined it was necessary, we
have changed names, details, and determining characteristics of
people.

Dedication

This short read is dedicated to the sacrifices made by our country's Founding Fathers, who pledged their lives, fortunes, and sacred honors for liberty. They promised to each other that they would "hang together," knowing that they were all at risk of "hanging separately" for treason.

Table of Contents

Chapter 1: Lawyering in a New World

There is no "justice system" in this country. We have a legal system, or, even more accurately stated, a dispute resolution system. "Justice" is for idealists and philosophers. *Law is war, and the attorneys and litigants are the combatants.* This little metaphor of mine is one that I recite frequently in my podcasts, and it never had more practical significance than on February 10th and 11th of 2016.

My name is Mike Arnold, and I am a criminal defense attorney who specializes in complex cases. I am the managing partner of an eight-attorney firm located in Eugene, Oregon, almost two hours south of Portland and five hours west of Burns, Oregon and the Malheur National Wildlife Refuge, the location of 2016's "Oregon Standoff" protest. My firm was retained by Ammon Bundy to represent him when he was arrested before the conclusion of the occupation.

This protest, which became known as the "Oregon Standoff," was of a particular interest to me and my firm, given its constitutional free speech/civil disobedience implications and its proximity to our law office. I followed it avidly, along with the other lawyers in my firm. As the protest went on, it was clear to me that the protesters needed the benefit of counsel, so I approved the request of two of my associate attorneys to drive out to the Refuge to offer *pro bono* (free of charge) assistance.

Once Ammon Bundy retained my firm to represent him in the post-arrest federal criminal case, I made many lifelong friends and more than a few enemies – all through my efforts to provide high-quality legal assistance and advice to my new client and friend. People loudly and publicly denounced our involvement as Ammon's attorneys even as we simply tried to provide to him the services he was constitutionally entitled to, services that my firm provides to our other clients on a daily basis. The naysayers didn't deter us, but it did provide me with insight into the disconnect between the citizens of this country and its legal system.

The Oregon Standoff gave a voice to many in this country who generally labor in silence — ranchers and farmers. Many have had plenty to say in support of the actions of Ammon and the other protestors, and have said it loudly. However, in my experience, the citizens most vocal about the legal system are actually unquestioning cheerleaders for the government. I have observed in my practice that most citizens outside of the legal system first presume guilt rather than innocence. I have also observed a complete lack of empathy for those involved in the legal system and their families. The legal system as it stands will continue to breed injustice if we allow ourselves to be swept into the mindset of blind retribution, a result that presumes guilt, rather than blind justice and the presumption of innocence.

Why has this happened? The process and its participants are seldom personalized to members of the community. Generally, the stories of people charged with crimes are not told because most citizens do not possess the resources to hire an attorney who can take the time to learn them and tell them. It is only by personalizing those in the legal system and telling their stories of injustice does change become a possibility. It's about changing one's frame of reference: Don't buy what the government is selling. Call the system what it is – a legal system – rather than calling it what it is not: a system of justice.

For lawyers, the legal system can seem abstract; we're dealing with incidents long after they have been completed, after the tense moments of the alleged criminal conduct has become a memory to the victims and the participants. Our work often takes place several months after the alleged criminal acts have long since been completed. However, that was not the case on the afternoon of January 27, 2016, when Arnold Law co-counsel Lissa Casey and I went on national television to ask the remaining protesters at the Malheur Refuge to "please stand down." We asserted ourselves right in the middle of the Oregon Standoff the day after LaVoy Finicum's shooting and minutes after we began representing Ammon Bundy as his lawyers in his federal criminal case and into the criminal injustice system.

As a trial lawyer, I seek to change this system one juror at a time, one cross examination question at a time, and as an author and podcast host, one reader or listener at a time. During the winddown of the final stand down in the Oregon Standoff, we were literally trying to save lives, one protester at a time.

Chapter 2: Telling What Story?

Telling the story of what has been called the "Oregon Standoff" has one major difficulty: where to begin? For Ammon Bundy, the story might begin at his family's ranch near Bunkerville, Nevada, where he and his family stared down militant Bureau of Land Management (BLM) agents during what has been called the "Bundy Standoff."

In a dispute over grazing and water rights going back decades, the BLM requested and received a court order requiring Cliven Bundy to remove his cattle from "federal lands." There was no court order permitting BLM to seize or kill cattle.

The position of Cliven Bundy (Ammon's father) was one that harkens me back to Day One of my Property Law class at the University of Oregon School of Law. The concept is called "the bundle of rights" or "bundle of sticks." These terms are a simple way of conceptualizing the complex nature of real property rights that any piece of real property inherently has connected to it. Various property rights, or sticks, can be assigned or sold off while retaining others. For instance, a person may keep an interest in a property to physically live there but could sell the grazing rights or mineral rights to someone else. He would still have the ability to physically occupy the property so long as that occupation didn't interfere substantially with the mining or ranching rights that were previously assigned to another.

Cliven saw his interest in "federal lands" as being one of grazing and water rights. He went toe-to-toe with the BLM agents who killed and seized many of his cattle until the federal government eventually backed down and released the surviving cattle. He and the hundreds of other protesters that supported him claimed a victory and went back to business as usual on the ranch. Thereafter, Cliven began referring to the Bundy Ranch as "the freest place on earth," given that the federal government thereafter left them alone.

For the next 21 months, there was no indication that any criminal prosecutions would occur resulting from the Bundy Standoff in Nevada. Many believe this lack of action by the federal government emboldened the Bundy family, leading to Ammon's choice to take his protest to Oregon.

While many might consider that "emboldenment" as the beginning of the Oregon protest, Ammon himself might consider "the beginning" to be the day he received a call from his father about the Hammonds, a ranching family in Harney County, Oregon, the largest county in Oregon and yet the fifth least populous of our 36 counties. Harney County, if it were a state, would be ranked 42nd in landmass ahead of Maryland, Vermont, New Hampshire, and others.

The beginning of this story for most onlookers and media was on January 2, 2016, the day that the occupation of the Malheur National Wildlife Refuge began.

For my law firm, the story began on January 8, 2016, when Arnold Law attorney Lissa Casey told me she was worried about the safety of the protesters in eastern Oregon and wanted to go out there and volunteer to help *pro bono*.

For me, the story really began January 27, 2016, the morning Lissa and I drove to Portland to advise Ammon Bundy after his arrest, the morning of his arraignment in United States District Court in downtown Portland.

Chapter 3: Why Harney County – the plight of the Hammonds

In October of 2015, Ammon Bundy was at home near Emmett, Idaho, when his dad called him and alerted him to the Hammond family's fight with the BLM. They both saw immediate similarities to the Bundy family's own fight with the BLM.

Ammon's interest in the case was sparked and he began researching it in earnest. He learned that the patriarch of the Hammond family, Dwight, and his son Steven had been arrested and convicted of arson. They were charged under the 1996 Antiterrorism and Effective Death Penalty Act, which was passed as a result of the 1993 World Trade Center and 1995 Oklahoma City bombings. Their alleged act of "arson" was, according to the Hammonds, a back burn set to protect their own property from a BLM-lit fire. The way the government charged the Hammonds under this misapplied terrorism statute subjected them to a mandatory minimum sentence of five years without any discretion of the sentencing judge.

At the sentencing hearing, soon-to-be-retiring Senior District Court Judge Michael Hogan of Eugene, Oregon, found that the mandatory minimum sentence violated the Cruel and Unusual Punishment Clause of the 8th Amendment due to it being disproportionate to the convicted crime. He found that the five-year sentence "shocked the conscience" and instead sentenced Dwight to three months and Steve to one year.

The government appealed the sentence and during the pendency of the appeal, the Hammonds served Judge Hogan's sentence and were released from prison to return to Harney County. The Ninth Circuit Court of Appeals reversed Judge Hogan's ruling and ordered a resentencing to the mandatory minimum. On October 7, 2015, Judge Ann Aiken sentenced the Hammonds to serve the remainder of the five-year mandatory sentence, and ordered them to report to the custody of the Bureau of Prisons in January 2016.

When Ammon Bundy learned about what happened and what the Hammonds' defense had been, he was appalled. He prayed on what to do and decided to act. He drove the three hours from his Idaho home to the Hammonds' ranch to meet with the family. He heard their account first hand and offered his support. His support was not just the pledge of one man but was effectively a pledge of support from an entire family clan and potentially a pledge from an entire political movement — a movement that has been described as the "Liberty" or "Patriot" Movement.

Ammon then and there decided to exercise his constitutional rights to help the Hammonds. He knew from his family's life-long study of the Constitution as well as the religious emphasis of the Constitution found in his LDS faith that there were several routes to effectuate change. Several of those tools were expressly outlined in the First Amendment, particularly the right to free speech and the right to petition the government for a redress of grievances.

Also, ingrained in Ammon and his family's belief about the rights of the people is that a county sheriff is the last line of defense to stand between the federal government and the people. Consequently, his initial main audience was with Harney County Sheriff Dave Ward. Ammon contacted the sheriff and others in the county asking them to stand with the Hammonds to protect them from the seizure by the federal government. He reached out to federal representatives and senators as well. He organized petitions, phone calls and email campaigns.

Ultimately, he was disappointed with the lack of support by the elected officials. It was then that phase two of his campaign for the Hammonds began. Unbeknownst to a steady-growing group of Hammond supporters who made their way to Burns, Oregon in a cold November and December, Ammon had a plan to bring national attention to the Hammonds' plight and to his family's long battle: a plight of government overreach that they perceived being brought down on individual citizen ranchers.

He decided to use the Fourth Estate as a tool of change. He was resolved to make a political stand that would bring public and national attention to this problem as did his father's stand in 2014. He would use the Freedom of the Press found in the First Amendment to achieve a national stage for him, the Hammonds, and the loosely organized "Liberty" or "Patriot" Movement.

As the Hammonds' January 4th surrender date loomed, on January 2, 2016, a protest was held at the Safeway in Burns, Oregon. At that protest, Ammon announced that he planned to make a harder stand than the protest's intended march to the fairgrounds. He announced that he intended to head to the Malheur National Wildlife Refuge to take it over. This Refuge was run by the United States Fish and Wildlife Service. While not the same entity as the BLM, both the refuge and BLM are arms of the Department of Interior.

Ammon and a small group of protesters headed to the Refuge. What happened on their arrival is corroborated by several witnesses but the details are greatly disputed by the FBI.

It was a holiday weekend and no employees were at the Refuge. After its vacancy was confirmed by a search of the buildings, Ammon Bundy posted a video-recorded plea on YouTube, where he announced that they had taken over the Refuge. He said, "We're calling people out here to come and stand. We need you to bring your arms and we need you to come to the Malheur National Wildlife Refuge."

And thus began the Armed Occupation of the Malheur National Wildlife Refuge, the Oregon Standoff.

For 24 days, Ammon Bundy held daily press conferences and anyone and everyone was free to come and go. At one point, Ammon Bundy even left the Refuge to meet with the FBI agents, where he shook their hands. He was never asked to leave by the federal government or told that his actions were perceived by them as being felonious. He and many others assumed that their actions were not criminal at all, but were a form of civil disobedience — at the most misdemeanor criminal trespass.

My firm followed the events closely. After a week of the protest, my Arnold Law colleague Lissa Casey approached me and said she was concerned that the federal government would overreact similar to Ruby Ridge or Waco. She told me that she believed the protesters were polite citizens who didn't appear to be interested in violence. Her concern was that the mere presence of firearms at the Refuge would invite a violent response from our modern-day militarized law enforcement.

She was also concerned that she was seeing potential Oregon state crimes in the news. Her biggest legal worry was the use of government vehicles. The mere operation of a government truck or heavy equipment could be considered Unlawful Use of a Vehicle – car theft. While not a serious felony, under Oregon's Repeat Property Offender Statute, after the government proves any one act of theft, each subsequent act (i.e., each time a truck or other vehicle is driven), a mandatory minimum sentence of 18 months results. Under an aid and abet theory, everyone involved in the protest could potentially be liable even if they didn't personally operate the vehicles. She worried that the ostensible leader, Ammon Bundy, appeared to be at the most risk.

Her comment to me was that this appeared to be a disagreement between the protesters and their government, which was largely constitutional in nature. They were espousing theories of government land ownership rooted in Article 1, Section 8, clause 17 of the United States Constitution.

She was disturbed that no local, central or eastern Oregon lawyers were offering *pro bono* legal services to help negotiate an exit strategy for the protest.

On January 8, 2016, I had just returned from a hearing involving a murder case in Hood River, Oregon. It was a stressful hearing with a lot on the line for my falsely accused client, particularly since the case was going to air on CBS's *48 Hours* prior to our trial date. I rolled back into Eugene and was immediately approached by Lissa. She asked if I would approve of her going to Harney County to meet with Ammon Bundy. She wanted to know what it would take to do that given the ethical limitations on a lawyer soliciting a potential client.

I explained to her that there was no prohibition against giving *pro bono* advice, but that we could and should assume that opponents of the protest would complain to the Oregon State Bar once this was discovered due to either political reasons or simply due to ignorance of our constitutionally protected "right to counsel."

I told her therefore to be very public about it and to protect our firm with a letter of solicitation, a method permitted by the Oregon State Bar for soliciting clients for money (even though we weren't). Our ethics counsel, Peter Jarvis, called this the "belt and suspenders" approach: free legal advice was the belt, but the letter, which wasn't necessary, was the suspenders. I quickly drafted the letter with his help and sent Lissa and another Arnold Law attorney out the door on a Friday evening. When she left, I told her that my only conditions for paying for the trip and assuming the professional liability was that she drive a 4x4 truck and keep her head down if there was a firefight. She agreed.

Lissa traveled to Burns and the Refuge. After driving for hours, her meeting with Ammon Bundy only lasted about 5 minutes. He said, "You guys are my lawyers but I think the people of Harney County need you more than I do right now. I will be in contact soon." Lissa returned home without incident.

Little did anyone know that soon Ammon's role in the occupation protest would be over and a new phase of his protest would begin in the courts. A few weeks after Lissa's trip to the Refuge, on January 26, 2016, a caravan of vehicles that Ammon was part of was ambushed by the Oregon State Police and FBI. The protesters were armed with overhead projectors, other educational implements, and a few firearms on their way to Grant County, Oregon to give a lecture on the Constitution.

During the ambush, Ammon and those in the vehicle he was in were quickly apprehended without incident, including the government informant driving the vehicle that helped set up the ambush. However, the stop of the vehicle driven by LaVoy Finicum did not go as smoothly. Finicum's truck was shot with what the FBI called a "less lethal" round. It was a 35 MM gas canister that was shot at the roof of Fincium's truck canopy. To the protesters in the truck, they had no way to know it was not a live round and thus an unlawful use of force. Finicum informed the agents that he was heading to the Grant County Sheriff to turn himself in and invited them to follow. Follow they did, pushing Finicum around a blind curve to a snowdrift-obscured roadblock, another ambush.

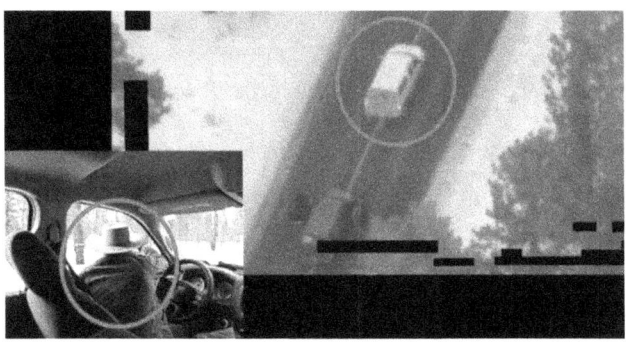

(Lavoy Finicum communicating with agents before the "Deadman's Roadblock.")

After rounding the corner and before Finicum's reaction time would have registered the imminent roadblock, the Oregon State Police fired live rifle rounds at the men and women in Finicum's truck. He attempted to drive to the left around the roadblock but got the truck stuck in the snow. He opened the door and was immediately fired upon by elite federal sharpshooters who either missed by accident or on purpose, hoping to provoke the protesters or the state police. These same federal agents later reportedly covered up their involvement by hiding their spent shell casings and lying to state investigators about their shots fired. At the time of the release of this book, the status of that criminal investigation is still unknown, cloaked in government secrecy.

Finicum left the truck, reportedly to draw fire away from the two women and one man left inside.

What happened next is largely in dispute and impossible to ascertain with certainty due to the fact that the government agents intentionally refused to wear body cameras and to activate their in-car video cameras. Our understanding of the incident is also clouded by the government-biased evidence released and what they chose not to release.

Ultimately, Finicum was shot and left to bleed to death in the snow while the agents pummeled the truck with a barrage of shots of pepper gas rounds. After the final occupants of the truck surrendered, thus began Stage Two of Ammon's protest: the Federal Court.

(Photo: Screenshot of the lone [known] FBI video of Lavoy with his hands up seconds before he is shot.)

(Photo: Lavoy shot and killed by Oregon State Police.)

The next morning, I was at home getting caught up on farm chores. Taking a break from real work, I headed into the office to make the rounds. Lissa approached me right away and notified me of the arrests of some of the protestors and death of Finicum. She suggested that we go up to Portland immediately to advise Ammon. We hopped in my black Ford pickup truck and headed to the Multnomah County Jail in the clothes that we were wearing. Luckily she was wearing a suit, but I was stuck in my farm clothes — muddy jeans and a dirty work-ravaged t-shirt.

After meeting with Ammon and working out a game plan, Lissa headed to the Federal Courthouse for arraignment while I went clothes shopping for a TV-appropriate suit. The plan was for me to make an announcement for Ammon after court to his supporters, his family, and to the protesters remaining at the Refuge.

I suited up and after court went out to the courthouse steps, where I was ambushed by dozens of media reps with their mics and cameras. I read Ammon's statement to them from my laptop that Ammon, Lissa and I fashioned together: "I'm asking the federal government to allow the people at the Refuge to go home without being prosecuted. To those remaining at the Refuge, I love you. Let us take this fight from here. Please stand down. Please stand down. Go home and hug your families. This fight is ours for now in the courts. Please go home."

After that message, all but four of the remaining protesters did stand down. Several were arrested on their way out or arrested in the days and weeks to follow. All that remained at the Refuge were the final four protester holdouts: Jeff Banta, Sean Anderson, Sandy Anderson and David Fry. They were left over in an information vacuum hyped up on rumors of Finicum's execution and an impending Waco-style FBI assault on the Refuge. However, that assault never happened. The FBI remained elusive and distant, perhaps attempting to lull the final four into complacency.

From that day on, Lissa and I made it our personal goal to assist in a peaceful ending for the final four in any way we could.

Chapter 4: The Final Four

Somebody call assembly woman Michele Fiore from Nevada!

Those were the pleading words of the final four protesters from the Malheur Refuge in Oregon. On February 10, 2016 the FBI laid siege on the final protesters' encampment at the Refuge. This was in Harney Country, Oregon, a vast high-mountain desert, winter wasteland of sage brush, rocks, and barbed wire. Three men and one woman were the only ones left.

An intense live feed was organized and broadcasted by political activist Gavin Seim. You could hear the terror in their voices as the final four pleaded for their lives. In fact, you can still go back and listen to these difficult moments, because Seim archived this all on his YouTube site\ (**http://snip.ly/gavinseim**) for the protection of the final four protesters that were holed up at the Refuge.

The "final four" as they were called, were David Fry of the Cincinnati, Ohio area, Jeff Banta of Elko, Nevada, and Sean and Sandy Anderson of Riggins, Idaho. They had remained at the Refuge after the killing of LaVoy Finicum, even though the other remaining protesters fled in disarray fearing an imminent attack at the Refuge.

By January 27th, the day of our plea from the courthouse steps, these four individuals were left alone on the Refuge to fend for themselves. Until the evening of February 10th, the FBI had been at a stalemate with these final four hold-outs. However, that all changed when the FBI drove up in "BearCat" armored vehicles and encircled the camp of the final four. This is the story of the last hours of the Oregon Standoff, as told by some of the participants: Mike Arnold, Lissa Casey, and Michele Fiore. What follows is an edited transcript of the re-telling, which was originally aired on a Law is War Podcast.

An Interview with Michele Fiore

Mike Arnold: We have with us today Michele Fiore. She's an assembly woman with the Nevada state legislature. Thanks for coming on the air, Michele.

Michele Fiore: Thanks for having me, I missed you guys.

Mike Arnold: Yeah, it's great to have you back in Oregon.

Michele Fiore: I know, I know!

Mike Arnold: So, you're talking to us from Portland. You are preparing to testify at the Ammon Bundy/Oregon protest trial and have a little break before your testimony. You graciously volunteered to come on the air. Why don't you introduce yourself and give us a little background about yourself.

Michele Fiore: Well, my name is Michele Fiore and I live in Las Vegas, Nevada. I'm the assembly woman for District 4. I have two grown beautiful girls and four grandkids. I'm definitely an advocate for our citizens. I believe that the Bureau of Land Management has been terrorizing the Western states for a while and I learned that first-hand in Nevada, in Bunkerville, in 2014.

Mike Arnold: So, you have first-hand knowledge of the Bunkerville-Bundy standoff that occurred against the BLM; you went out there and made some observations.

Michele Fiore: Oh, yes. I was on the ground for 14 days, driving back and forth from my home to Bunkerville. You know as a mom, when your kids say: 'Hey Mom, there is a monster under my bed,' you go in their room and you show them there's no monster; you look under their bed and you show them there's nothing there.

So, when people were calling me about Bunkerville and the Bureau of Land Management killing cows and tazing people and kidnapping people, I literally went out there with a frame of mind that I'm going to show them that this is not our government, this is not our Bureau of Land Management. I got out there and I literally witnessed and saw some horrific monsters at the BLM. They have turned into a bureaucracy and an agency of terrorists themselves. I could not believe our federal government and our elected officials in Washington and the States were allowing this type of behavior to their citizens. And that's when I took my first stand.

Mike Arnold: What happened in 2016 that got you involved at the Refuge?

Michele Fiore: In 2016, there were ranchers up here in your state, in Oregon. Steven Hammond and his family. The BLM was terrorizing them and I thought to myself, you know...there are elected officials, they'll fix this and get them straightened out. However, Ammon Bundy, who I'm just going to tell you, he is the greatest individual and you know when they say: Love thy neighbor and protect thy neighbor...He is an example. When he found out about the situation, he ignored it at first. Then something came over him and he felt compelled to go meet him and maybe give him some education on what they've learned.

He went and met with the Hammonds. He did a protest out there in Burns and he was hoping that the Sheriff out there, Sheriff Ward, would step up and say, "Sorry, BLM, but you're not taking this man to jail." And that didn't happen. So, a lot of men that stood in Bunkerville went to Oregon to Burns to sit with the Hammonds. And that's how I got involved in Oregon with the Hammonds and all that.

(Photo: Michele with Ammon Bundy in 2014).

Mike Arnold: Did you come out to Oregon to visit?

Michele Fiore: No, I did not come to Oregon to visit. I had one telephone call. I was patched in by the telephone call to the meeting between some of the Harney County elected officials, some FBI, the judge, and some other elected officials as well as folks from the Coalition of Western States that were there. I couldn't make the meeting; I was in Nevada with several meetings on my agenda for that day. But, when I did come to Oregon, it was after they got arrested – Ammon Bundy and Ryan Bundy. I came to Oregon to meet with Mike Arnold to see as to how and why my boys are in jail, why they are in Portland and how do we get them out.

So that's when I came to Oregon and that was a historical evening. The cell service on my phone was going off. Then, I met superhero, Mike Arnold, and it was just amazing.

Mike Arnold: So, basically, Ammon invited you and other elected officials to come out to Oregon to have a meeting and a press conference to talk about some of the issues that he was interested in that led him to the protest in Oregon. You had flown out intending to do that and what changed?

Michele Fiore: The thing that changed was that the Federal Government was surrounding the last four individuals that were in the Refuge and they were basically about to kill them. Flat out murder. I don't know how else to say that; there is nothing politically correct that I should say. I can't lighten that verb. Facts are facts. Thank goodness for technology, because we got patched through to them, to the last four with Sean and Sandy Anderson, David Fry and Jeff Banta.

Mike Arnold: Let back up and put this into context. So, the end of January, Ammon Bundy and several other leaders of the protest were arrested and the next day they were arraigned in federal court. After the arraignment, Lissa Casey and I went on the courthouse steps and read a statement from Ammon Bundy, saying: "To the folks that were left on the Refuge, please stand down and go home and be with your families."

At that point, more people had left the Refuge. And over the course of several days, there was nobody left at the Refuge, except for what we have grown to call "the final four." Now, give us those names, of the final four.

Michele Fiore: So, the final four were: Shawn and Sandy Anderson, Jeff Banta and David Fry.

Mike Arnold: And then, you had flown in...You were landing at the Portland International Airport. You finally were allowed to turn on your phone and then what happened next?

Michele Fiore: The phone blew up. I mean, they were trying to get me while I was in the air. When I say "they" I am talking about the final four, the last four that were standing. And Gavin Seim was trying to patch me through. Deb Jordan was calling, because they were calling her.

Mike Arnold: Deb Jordan is Pete Santilli's partner in life and also with the broadcast "The Pete Santelli Show."

Michele Fiore: Yes, absolutely. Deb Jordan is actually an amazing…an amazing individual. So, the only thing I had to write a phone number down with was a sharpie. So, I took the sharpie pen and wrote the number to be patched in on my wrist and that number from that sharpie was on my wrist for two days.

So, that's how we got patched in. From that phone call – the minute I was patched in – my phone was dying. I was in the back of the plane. The other passengers on the plane thought I was insane as I'm telling them, "Calm down; no one's gonna kill you. Tell the FBI to get on the phone." I mean, imagine being on an airplane, and this woman is on the phone, talking to the last four and trying to convey messages to a very zealous FBI negotiator.

Mike Arnold: At some point, I was driving up to the airport to pick you up. We were going to go prep for the next morning's meeting. We were going to meet with Ammon Bundy at the jail. Lissa, why don't you say what happened next?

Lissa Casey: Well, I wasn't in Portland that night. I was at home in Eugene. And I saw that there was this live feed going on and I started tuning in and I texted you: "You need to start listening to this." And, I knew you were on your way to pick up Michele. So, once the live feed happened, they were demanding to speak with Michele out at the Refuge.

Mike Arnold: Why? What happened?

Lissa Casey: Well, the day that Michele flew in, I guess rather the evening, they [FBI] rolled in BearCats and started surrounding the Refuge.

(Photo: A Lenco BearCat armored vehicle, euphemistically labeled a "rescue vehicle.")

Mike Arnold: And they did this knowing that Michele Fiore was on her way. And while she was in the air, the FBI took BearCats, which are armored vehicles, and moved in on the final four, who were basically left unmolested for at least two weeks after the protest ended.

Lissa Casey: And the big fear of the final four was that after LaVoy Finicum was killed, they were going to be killed too, and so they started holing up; and the dynamic of everything really changed after what happened to LaVoy.

Mike Arnold: I think they told us on the phone, because we had spoken to them a couple of days earlier and they said, "Look, we're out here for ourselves now." It wasn't any protest anymore…they were scared for their lives.

Lissa Casey: They were. Because they were turned into this, you know. You have to imagine what it was like for them out there. Because I remember when we were trying to speak with them through Gavin Seim – he patched us in, when we were with Lisa Bundy. They're trying to talk and stay calm and Mike is trying to talk and get them counsel and try to arrange for if they were to surrender, that they would have legal counsel ready and waiting, and we had that.

(Photo: A screenshot from the video Mike, Lissa and Lisa Bundy recorded for the final four on January 29, 2016).

But, they were scared because, even before they did the BearCats, when they were talking with Mike, they kept telling us that there were drones, there were drones. And we were going, "Where are the drones? What are you talking about, with the drones?"

So, we got on the phone with the FBI agent and it was like the right hand didn't know what the left hand was doing, because the FBI agent we were talking to said, there's no drones. And Mike is going, "There are drones out there. They're telling us, 'There are drones.' Bring them back. How can I negotiate with these people, when there's drones out there?"

And then, sure enough, the FBI agent found out that there were drones out there. It was similar with Michele: how can we negotiate with these people, when you've brought BearCats in this situation? There was a lot of fear injected in this situation that night on the part of the final four.

Mike Arnold: At that point, it turned out a little different than what Michele and I had planned. What happened next, in terms of getting ahold of you, Michele?

Lissa Casey: This is my favorite part of the journey.

Mike Arnold: Let's go through this a little more chronological. So, I'm getting these frantic messages from Lissa that they've rolled. What's going on in my mind is, "Oh no, this is going to sort of spark some sort of fire fight and these people's lives are in danger." Perhaps, the FBI is in danger. What if the FBI with their BearCats provokes some sort of crazy gunshot…they're gonna move in? You know, we didn't know if these fears were rational. We didn't know anything.

Lissa Casey: But, I was listening to the live feed at home and I thought those fears were rational. I remember, talking to you and you were telling me that you and Michele were trying to get to Burns. I had a child to take care of and I remember I called my mom and I told her to come over. I said if we don't get out there, these people might die. We have to go, we have to do this. I started driving up I-5 north.

Mike Arnold: So, I had the contact information from Audrey at the FBI. I texted her at 5:59 PM on Wednesday, February 10th, saying, "Fiore is landing. Can you get her on the phone with them?" meaning the final four.

I said, "I'm listening to the live stream. She offered to talk to them and the offer remains open. They are asking to speak to Fiore, right now. We can make it happen. We can slow this down. Tell them this doesn't have to be a military operation. We can slow it down by offering Michele Fiore to talk to them."

What I was conveying is that it doesn't need to be a military operation by the FBI. Then, I texted Audrey from the FBI, "There are still ways to negotiate this, without using force." And, then, at 6:11 PM. I ask, "Can someone pass them the word that Michele Fiore will talk to them, but they need to put their guns down. There doesn't need to be bloodshed and she's willing to talk with them about how to diffuse this right now."

I was wanting the FBI to convey to the final four: "Hey, we're in the circle here. We all understand what's going on. Michele Fiore is here to help diffuse the situation." I wanted candor and faith amongst the negotiators. Then, I say, "The Courts are there to defend them." I wanted the FBI to pass on that information from Michele and me. And then I say, "She can encourage them to stand down and step up to the next phase of their protest in the courts. Get the negotiators and the FBI back in charge; this isn't a military campaign."

Then, finally, I get a text message back from Audrey and she says, "I have passed your messages on." This is a very dynamic situation. I finally arrive at the Portland airport. You know, I've been there a couple of times. I park in their big garage. I think I grabbed my briefcase and my cellphone and I start running into the airport. And I don't even know how to get ahold of Michele. I don't know if she's at baggage claim; I don't know at what terminal she's at and I can't call her, because she's actually on the phone with the final four protestors.

Lissa Casey: Through the live feed...

Mike Arnold: Through the live feed. So, basically, I couldn't listen to the live feed because every time I listen to it, it's on YouTube. I wouldn't be able to text or make phone calls.

So, Lissa is texting me what's going on at that time and then finally I start communicating with Gavin Seim, who's on the phone with the final four. I communicated through his brother Nathan, because Gavin couldn't communicate with me, either. So, what happened there, Lissa?

Lissa Casey: Well, then you and Michele find each other, while Michele's on the live feed.

Mike Arnold: Yeah, we're communicating over the live feed. I'm telling Nathan where I am. Nathan is telling Gavin where I am. And then Gavin is telling Michele. Michele tells where she is and he passes the message over the live feed for the media to hear. I start looking for her, and finally I find her. At the same time, folks in the media are listening and they're thinking, "Well, let's go to the airport and take a look at this."

Lissa Casey: This is one of my favorite parts of the night, because you find Michele, and I remember the next day seeing pictures of you guys just sitting at the airport, trying to figure this out. You're on your cellphone, Michele's on her cellphone and you're talking to the final four.

Mike Arnold: Actually, there's passersby; there's tons of people. Man, I get there and Michele tells me her cellphone is dying. And this is a disaster…we don't know if Michele gets off the phone is everything going to be disrupted…if the final four are going to do something that antagonizes the FBI, or if the FBI's going to antagonize them. So, we don't want to lose this connection.

Lissa Casey: This connection is what's keeping both sides from fearing each other, at this point. Because you have FBI negotiators and BearCats on one side, and four really scared people that think they are about to die on the other side. I mean, I'll never forget how David Fry sounded on the live feed. And Michele on the live feed is what's keeping these two sides at bay, at this point. And she's pretty much the only thing that's doing it.

Mike Arnold: What happens when I run into you? Where were we at? When do we finally get hold of each other at the airport, Michele?

Michele Fiore: I was outside looking for you. I see you running towards me and I'm like, there's Mike! And then, we get inside and you get my cellphone plugged in.

Mike Arnold: So, I grab you by the arm. I take you to the airport. There was a gentleman at the kiosk who was very helpful. I said, "She is on the phone with the final four protestors at the Malheur Refuge. If her phone dies, somebody might die at the Refuge. Please, help us find an outlet." We didn't have a cord, either. So, someone got us a cord. They find us an outlet, we plugged you in and we just sat down on the floor while you were on the phone and I'm texting the FBI trying to coordinate.

(Photo: Mike listening to Michele talk to the final four while charging the phone at Portland International Airport).

Basically, I wanted them to stand down. I wanted the FBI to back off. So, I'm trying to communicate with them. I asked the airport police if they could get us a private room at the airport, like a conference room to help us and they refused to help. By then, there is a video camera from I believe it was KOIN or KGW or one of the local Portland affiliates and John Sepulvado from OPB (Oregon Public Broadcasting) shows up. Somebody walks by and says to him, "What's going on here?"

And he makes a snide-ass comment to the walker-by and says, "Oh, they're just doing this to get media attention."

I was like, "Fuck you." So, I grabbed Michele and said, "Let's get the fuck out of here." I grab her by the arm and this OPB troll has got his cellphone out and he's recording me as we're walking away. You know, saying we're doing this for the media. We're trying to get away from the media. At this time, I don't realize that everybody is listening on the live feed. You know, as far as I know, it's like five other people.

Lissa Casey: There were tens of thousands of people listening to this and in true Mike Arnold fashion, his solution is, he literally walks out of the airport then flags down [transport]. [As of December 13, 2016, the recorded "live feed" had been listened to 1,310,785 times.]

Mike Arnold: Well, you know, I see somebody in a pickup truck, and I think, Okay. Pickup truck. That's probably going to be someone…you know, it was a beat up pickup truck…I'm like, they're going to want to help somebody out. I'm not going to go to the Prius who's going to run away and think that we're weird, because we're on the phone. We're acting kinda crazy. Let's not forget, we were jazzed up.

Lissa Casey: That's an understatement. This was a unique situation.

Mike Arnold: Yeah, I mean, it was really stressful. We didn't know what was going to happen. So, I run outside. I see this lady loading up her car and I say, "Hey, can we have a ride to the parking lot? We're trying to get away from these press people," and I point to the OPB troll. Then, I point to the camera. She says, "I don't know, why don't you ask my boyfriend?"

So, I open the door and I met Ray. I say, "Hey, Ray, can you give us a ride?" I explain to him what's going on. I don't know if I'm hyperbolic or what. People's lives are at stake. This is what I'm perceiving at that time.

He's says, "Yeah, hop on in." So, we hop in the car. We leave them in the dust, the folks at the airport. He takes us around the loop into the parking garage. Then, what do you do at this point? Are you still talking to them on the phone, Michele?

Michele Fiore: I'm still talking to them on the phone. You are handling everything. And I am still talking to them on the phone.

Mike Arnold: So, basically, I'm grabbing you by the arm and I'm pushing you into a car at this point.

Michele Fiore: Haha. Yes, yes.

Mike Arnold: Then, we get out. We're finally free from the vultures. We hop in the truck and I think I'm intending to go downtown to continue our plan, to meet and confer with some other elected officials. We're going to talk with Ammon. We just start driving downtown. At that point, I finally get this text message to talk to this Mark guy at the FBI. He finally calls me. I'm like, alright... I take the first exit. I need to pull over. It's this long straightaway. There's no place to pull over.

Michele Fiore: You pull over on the sidewalk.

Mike Arnold: Yeah. So, I pull over on the sidewalk. I'm just sitting there, talking to the FBI. What's going on at this point, Michele?

Michele Fiore: So, I'm thinking to myself... I don't think we're supposed to be on the sidewalk. But, I really have to focus on these four, that are sort of there and alive still. And I'm hearing the FBI in the background. And I gotta just focus on the four. So, I did not focus where we were, Mike. I knew you had all of that under control. I just knew that I didn't think we should be on the sidewalk. But, hey, lives are at stake here. So, I literally was on the phone and I'm trying to calm the FBI down and our last four standing there. And you were dealing with the FBI. We were talking about flying a helicopter. I just heard bits and pieces of what you were doing. And I was really, just trying to focus on the last four guys there.

Mike Arnold: Yeah. So, finally, I get a text message from the FBI. It says: "Mark is the best person to answer all of their questions. He has spoken to them over the last several weeks." I guess this is after I spoke to Mark. Mark tells me on the phone: "We need you to get to Burns. We need you to get to the Refuge. We want Michele out there to speak to the final four in person."

I say, "How do you want us to get there?

He says, "We're going fly you out. We're trying to get a helicopter or a flight out there."

He works on that and then calls me back and says, "Well, we can't get a helicopter right now. Can you get back to the airport and fly over to Redmond. And then, we'll get you a car or pick you up from there and drive you to Burns.

I say, "I think this is too complicated. We're just going to drive over." There was no sense of waiting for a commercial airline to fly me over the Cascades to central Oregon when I've got a four-wheel pickup and some free time while Michelle is on the phone. So, I put it back in gear and hop off the curb. And, I'm on the phone with the FBI. I'm say, "I don't even know where I am right now. I'm not a city driver. Like, where do I go?"

They reply, "Hold on." Then, Mark turns the phone over to somebody who's an Oregonian local and they tell me to get to some random highway that's close to the airport. They're trying to coordinate, basically, how to get there. Because, you know, I'm on the phone. I can't access directions on the iPhone.

Lissa Casey: GPS.

Mike Arnold: Yeah, the GPS. So, they're telling me how to get there. So, we hop on this lonely road and all of the sudden, we're driving up into the mountains. What's going on at this point, Michele?

Michele Fiore: We're driving like crazy people. Through the mountains. In the pouring rain. Lots of trees. Lots of curves. And, my life is in your hands.

Mike Arnold. In all fairness, every time we saw headlights... Because, at this point, it's a... It's dark... It's rainy, it's cloudy... It's the winter time in Oregon. And, every time I saw headlights, I would slam on the brakes carefully. And, I would slow us down. So, we never put anybody else in danger, other... You know... I put you in danger. If we ran into a tree or went off the road...But you know... We were driving safely around other people. But, we're in the middle of nowhere. I mean, there's no houses. There's nothing. We're just going through the mountains. You're chatting with the final four. I'm chatting with the FBI and I'm trying to negotiate a stand down, because everybody was tired. You've been on the phone quite some time and what we were really worried about was that cool heads wouldn't prevail and somebody was going to do something silly. So, I was trying to get the FBI to not invade the campground in the middle of the night. That's what everybody was worried about. They didn't want to get off the phone and go to sleep, because they were afraid the FBI was going to basically kill them in the middle of the night. You know, not necessarily invading with the intention to kill them. But, invade their final campground and then somebody is going to make a mistake and shots we're going to be fired.

Lissa Casey: The armored vehicles were really scaring David Fry the most out of all of them. He was the one who was on the feed and it got really intense at one point. He was saying, "They've got armored vehicles. They have their guns pointed at us. So just so you know, I'm ready to die. I'm gonna die tonight. I'm ready to die." He was that scared. This fear was real and the darkness exacerbated this situation. Each side didn't know what the other side was willing to do.

Mike Arnold: The next thing I get at 7:38 is a cellphone number for Mark at the FBI. I call; there's no answer. So, ultimately, I was able to through to Mark at the FBI. I was able to negotiate with them to basically not to do anything in the middle of the night, to stand down. I don't know if they pulled back the BearCats or what happened.

And just a funny little side note... At some point, you get mad at me, because you think I'm playing music on the stereo. Because, when I got off the phone with Mark at one point, my Bluetooth automatically engaged, the music started playing over the speaker really loud. And, you remember what that was, Michele?

Michele Fiore: Yeah. That song was crazy. It was some country song. I mean, it was perfectly soothing. But, I was like... that is something.

Mike Arnold: And, you remember what it was, Lissa?

Lissa Casey: Wasn't it "Country Boys Will Survive"?

Mike Arnold: Yeah. "A Country Boy Can Survive" by Hank Williams Jr. It was fitting for the moment.

Michele Fiore: Yeah...

Lissa Casey: In the meantime, while you guys are driving up east, I'm driving up north then driving out east to meet you guys.

Mike Arnold: Yeah. I tell you to come up to Portland. And, all of a sudden, I tell you we're going to Burns.

Lissa Casey: You literally texted me, "Turn right. Go to Burns." So, I did. I start into the mountains. In the meantime, Franklin Graham is in the air, he's flying out, because he'd been talking and praying with them throughout the week. So, we have Fiore and Franklin Graham on the way. But, at this point nobody really knows what's going to happen. That's why tens of thousands of people were tuning in, because it kept amping up and Michele would bring it back down. The thing that stuck out to me with Michele talking to them was, whenever the situation would get amped up, Michele would go: "Alright, it's time to pray" and she would pray with them and you could feel them come back.

Mike Arnold: Yeah. I remember sitting there next to her. Who else was on the line at that point, Michele?

Michele Fiore: Franklin came on the line with us a few times.

Mike Arnold: And, Gavin Sime, who was a political activist and kind of a provocateur of the Liberty movement. An articulate young man who does a lot of YouTube videos about freedom and liberty and tyranny. At some point, didn't KrisAnne Hall get on the line? Or was that the next day?

Michele Fiore: I'm not sure. I think it was the next day.

Mike Arnold: So, that night, it was this, you in and out with Franklin Graham and I was really impressed when you would take these breaks, like Lissa mentioned. Because I can hear the tension in your voice and I would keep telling you things, right? What would I say to you as we were driving?

Michele Fiore: God, if you just had a camera in your car, Mike. Because, you were truly, were the director and the facilitator. A lot of people give me credit. But, I have to give that credit to you and Gavin and… And the four. Because we all work together and make sure we didn't have a little weight go on our hands.

Mike Arnold: Every time I hear you voice get all tense, I would redirect you and tell you to calm them down. To do something. You break into a prayer. In the meantime, I'm on the phone with the FBI too. I'm saying. "Fucking give me some tips on how do to this. I have no negotiation training. What do we say? What do we do?"

Lissa Casey: Neither you nor Michele are professional negotiators. But, you are just thrown into this situation. All of the sudden, you're negotiating and doing what the FBI can't.

Mike Arnold: As a lawyer, I'm a professional negotiator. But, it's usually in high conflict criminal cases where nobody has guns, as far as I know.

Lissa Casey: It was in addition to you calming them down with prayer which still sticks out to me, you used humor in only the way Michele Fiore can. I think. You would say things to them like, "We're gonna put our big girl panties on when to take America back" and say these things to them in this completely intense situation with FBI negotiators and BearCats. But only, you were just being Michele. I think that's in the end why people give you so much credit because in a situation that you did not expect to be in, a situation of intensity that no one really expects to be in and you were just you and I think the final four felt that and they felt that you are just genuinely trying to help the situation and you were going to just be who you were and try to connect with them as much as you could and you did, in a very unconventional way. I don't know many FBI negotiators who would talk about big girl panties, taking America back. But, you did and you just connected with them and kept them sane and calm and you knew exactly what to do just because like you said you're a human being with a big heart. You were trying to empathize with them and trying to go with the flow of the situation, which was not easy.

Mike Arnold: We knew we were coming up to the pass and we knew that we were going to lose cellphone reception. I remember Michele telling the final four, "We're getting off the phone soon. Don't think anything bad has happened. It's all okay. We're going to go to the pass. Mike Arnold is driving his F150 really fast. We're going to get there to you." And, I'm talking to the FBI and I'm wanting some advice. I remember asking Lissa to Google "how to negotiate a hostage situation."

Lissa Casey: I was. I was texting Mike tips or trying to try to tell him to tell Michele to tell these people this.

Mike Arnold: So, she's texting me, "Step 1: build rapport. Step 2: do this and so on."

I'm getting these text messages from Lissa and I'm whispering to Michele, "Hey say this."

Lissa Casey: We are all learning how to negotiate an FBI situation on the fly.

Mike Arnold: Yeah. Because I'm on the phone with the FBI, periodically. And, I'm trying to get an agreement. Finally, I get a text message at 8:28 PM from an unknown FBI source and it reads, "Mark is the best person to answer all the questions. He spoke with them for the last several weeks. Fiore can call and check on them every hour or so to ensure the safety, giving her a chance to rest. They can always call her if they have a concern. Often best to have some down time to let emotions lower. We will take you both and Rev. Graham to Refuge around 8 AM. Believe they will all come out if both of them are there."

And then I say, "Who is this?"

He replies, "Mark with the FBI."

"Ok I'm telling her if she would shut up for a sec," I write.

She's doing her magic and finally she pauses and I tell her this and I text back to the FBI, " There's no way I get her off the phone right now, can you text me some intel?"

Finally, I get back on the phone with the FBI, thinking that we've got all the information. Michele communicates to them about something to the effect that, "Look, we're going to have a good night's sleep. The FBI's agreed to stand down."

And then finally, we lose reception. Everybody's got an agreement to stand down and we were no longer having to drive super fast. We slow down the truck and were just heading over to bed and then I get a text message from the FBI saying, "You know which hotel you guys are going to be staying at. I also need assembly woman's cell phone number."

Lissa Casey: Let me jump in because then, when that's happening to you, you text me and you just said, book us three hotel rooms. I'm like, okay boss. I'll do that. And, I'm driving through the mountains. I don't have a lot of cell reception. I'm trying to listen to the live feed. I have two cell phones. I remember that I took my mom's cell phone with me so I can have one cell phone for the live feed and one cell phone to be communicating with Mike.

Mike Arnold: Brilliant! Good idea!

Lissa Casey: And, I did. So we meet in the hotel lobby at the Doubletree. That's where I found rooms for us and we all meet in the lobby to convene and figure out a plan.

Mike Arnold: Let's not forget what we learned next.

Michele: Oh, my God. First of all, what people don't realize is before I jumped on the plane to get to Portland, I was on the phone with Cliven Bundy and Cliven was flying in too. He missed the flight that he was supposed to be on with me. He missed that flight. And we were going to meet with Ammon. Cliven was going to see Ammon and Ryan, to say, what next, boys? Like, what do we do next? So, I think about Cliven. What would have happened if Cliven was on the plane with me? Would we both have gone to jail, you know what I'm saying? It was just insane. So, when we get to the hotel, Carol, Cliven's wife calls me. She tells me he didn't get off the plane. And, I'm like, "What are you talking about? Cliven is missing? He didn't get off the plane?"

Through all of this, I totally forgot that when I got off the plane and I got with Mike Arnold that Cliven was going to be calling me when he landed and was going to be meeting with us, as well. And, because of all of the new emergencies, I just totally forgot that. So, when she said, Cliven is missing, then we went and we called, I think it was Mark, right? We called Mark at the FBI and said, "Where's Cliven?"

Mike Arnold: We say, "Where is he at?"

Mark checks into it, and he says, "Yeah, he's been arrested." And I flip out on the phone.

Lissa Casey: You do. You're like, really? Out of all the times to arrest Cliven Bundy, this is the time you're going to arrest. We just negotiated, calmed for the night and you thought this would de-escalate the situation. We just de-escalated it and you arrest Cliven Bundy. Now of all times.

Mike Arnold: I'm pissed, I'm yelling, I'm cursing. Mark is a professional negotiator and he is very good and he says, "Look, the negotiation team had nothing to do with it." It was like the left hand is not talking to the right hand.

Lissa Casey: That was consistent throughout.

Mike Arnold: It wasn't some vast conspiracy by the FBI. This is the way the government operates. It was why conspiracy theories, in my opinion, can never ever happen, because there is no vast sophistication in the government that can't even fix the goddamn potholes on the highway, you think they're going orchestrate some elaborate scheme to arrest Cliven Bundy.

Lissa Casey: Don't you always tell me, don't infer malice, when you can infer incompetence?

Mike Arnold: Yes. And that's Occam's Razor right there. The simplest explanation is usually the truest one. The fact is they had their hands full with the final four and in the meantime, the Las Vegas folks wanted Cliven.

Lissa Casey: So, they drafted a hurried complaint. Now, this is not an indictment, right? This is a criminal complaint that they arrest him on. I'm like, what in the world? Going through my head is that the final four are going to hear about Cliven and they are going to infer bad faith and this is going to set us back. So, we slow down and I talked to Carol Bundy on the phone and we all get our wits about us.

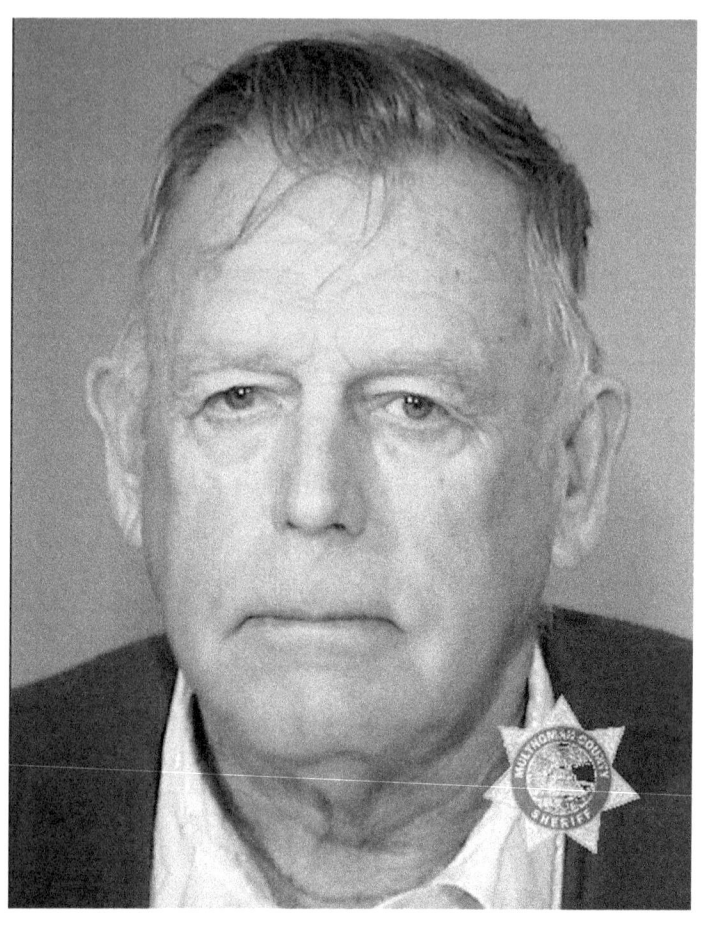

(Photo: Cliven Bundy's 2016 mugshot.)

Michele Fiore: Basically, I have to tell you Mike, that was our biggest, biggest, biggest concern, everything we just negotiated was going to be destroyed.

Mike Arnold: Yes. It was a big concern. So, we asked the folks from the Doubletree to make us some dinner.

Lissa Casey: We're all doing this in the lobby, by the way. We were on the phone with the FBI, in the hotel lobby and the clerks are like, who are these people.

Mike Arnold: They were nice enough to keep the restaurant open a little longer. I think we get some beverages and some food brought out to the lobby and we calmed down. We all go up to Michele's room and try to coordinate some things, because Michele was waiting for Shelley Shelton and some other folks at the Nevada Assembly to arrive.

(Photo: Michele Fiore in November 2016.)

Mike Arnold: Then we all go to bed and then the next morning we wake up super early and the FBI, three agents are waiting down in plain clothes in the lobby and you know, it's two men and a woman, right? It's Vinny, Jordan and you remember the girl's name?

Lissa Casey: I don't.

Michele Fiore: It think it's with a J.

Lissa Casey: They were not dressed like FBI agents. This is my first time actually just you know, 'Hello, FBI agents. Nice to meet you.' Shaking their hands and see that they're driving a red Kia.

Mike Arnold: I'm skeptical. I walk out and I see this red Kia and I expect a big, black Explorer or Expedition.

Lissa Casey: And we're like, where's our ride?

Mike Arnold: So, I make them show me their ID. So, I was like, is every black SUV in the entire Central and Eastern Oregon already rented by FBI? They're like, yeah... Pretty much. So, we hopped into my pickup truck. We pull in behind the Kia. Michele is trying toget the final four back on the line, right?

Michele Fiore: We get the final four back on the line, the fabulous four. We get them back on the line. And, we're on the phone with them and we don't want to lose connection. We don't want to lose connection.

Mike Arnold: We're driving east and were going to Burns and I'm told that it was an hour drive. So, we finally hit the road at six o'clock probably. We were driving east and Michele is talking to the final four. Think at this point, KrisAnne Hall gets on. Maybe Victoria Sharp at some point too and then, Gavin and Michele and I think this point Rev. Graham is in the air. He's flying his own personal jet. When I say flying, he's piloting his own personal jet. Not a prop plane, it's a screaming jet.

Lissa Casey: We were at the airport. We watched Graham fly and that was quite a sight.

Mike Arnold: Yeah. I didn't realize at that time with his hands on the stick.

Lissa Casey: I didn't either.

Mike Arnold: So, we're driving east. At some point Michele learns that the final four are getting agitated because we promised them we'd be there at the Refuge by 8 AM and it turns out the FBI didn't calculate the commute very well. I told Michele to let them know that it's not her fault, it's not the FBI's fault. It's just the drive and it's a little miscommunication.

(Photo: Discussing the plan with Michele on the way to Burns.)

Lissa Casey: And more importantly, nothing went wrong. We were still on our way. It's not the FBI saying Michele Fiore is coming and they're lying.

Mike Arnold: Yes. We diffuse that there. We're behind the Kia and they're going at a pretty good clip, right?

Lissa Casey: So, then Mike decides that he's gonna floor it and pass the FBI and I remember going, 'Mike I don't I don't think you should do this...Ok, ok, floor it.'

Mike Arnold: So, we start gunning past the FBI and I think we wave at them and we told them to follow us and we were going something like 100 miles an hour in the F150.

Lissa Casey: We're not putting anybody's lives in danger.There's no cars on the road.

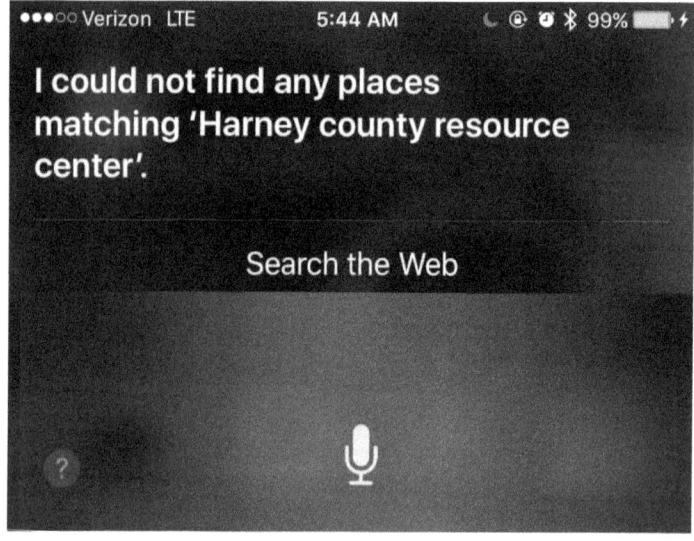

(Photo: Siri didn't laugh nor help us out when we asked for directions. "Harney County Resource Center" was what the protesters renamed the refuge.)

Mike Arnold: In fact, if we were to go off the on the side of the road, it would be sagebrush and a barb wire fence and with side impact airbags, I'm thinking it's pretty safe. So, we're going 100 miles an hour, there's no precipitation, no ice on the ground, there's snow everywhere on the side.

Lissa Casey: At all times, you can probably see 15 miles. I mean to describe the landscape out here, it's dramatic. It's totally barren. So, we're just going for it.

Mike Arnold: So, we zing past them. There's somebody else that we passed too. Then the little shitty Kia rental zips past us. I'm like, okay, I guess they probably have professional training on how to drive real fast and so we should just trust them.

(Photo: The view from the F150 as we followed the FBI Kia).

Lissa Casey: Eventually we stopped. We stopped and the FBI agent stopped. We were realizing it's really cold out there and we're going to wear hats and gloves, because probably we will be outside all day. At least, Michele will be.

Mike Arnold: Yes. We asked to stop at a little convenience store. We go in and I bought a bunch of gloves and hats.

Lissa Casey: And then, we come back out and as Michele's getting in the car with...

Mike Arnold: ...in the Kia?

Lissa Casey: No. In our truck. I remember you telling her earlier in the day, "You stay with me. If the FBI tries to go and take you, just stay with me." But, it all happened so fast.

Mike Arnold: Let's keep in mind, that we have little trust issue. I think mainly I'm going to blame Michele. Michele has a big trust issue with the FBI, because people were calling her co-conspirator. She was worried about being arrested. People were calling for Michele's arrest, for being on the phone with the folks at Harney County and communicating and so, there is a trust issue and so I told her to stay with us we're not going to leave you.

Lissa Casey: We just need to stay together. The FBI agents walk up to the passenger side of the truck. I'm sitting in the backseat, and it was the gal. She's like, 'Michele is coming with us.' We're like, 'No, she's going to stay here.' She responded, 'No you guys can't go any further, Michele is going to just come with us.'

Mike Arnold: But, that wasn't the agreement.

Lissa Casey: That was not the agreement, and Michele is like, 'Oh, okay.' It was just one of those things where we had a plan but all happened so fast. Michele gets out of the car and we're like, Michele is out of the car. And, they get her to the Kia so fast.

Mike Arnold: Isn't somebody from your assembly behind us too?

Lissa Casey: Yes.

Mike Arnold: Michele?

Michele Fiore: It was the assembly woman, Shelly Shelton, and John Moore. I had two assembly members from Nevada with me. Yeah. It was really kind of scary. It wasn't our plan. I don't know why they do things like that. It's just creates mistrust.

(Photo: Michele being whisked away by the FBI.)

Lissa Casey: Well, you guys were in separate cars because all of you were afraid you were getting arrested.

Mike Arnold: Yeah. You had an agreement with everybody never to travel together.

Lissa Casey: In a big group. So, then John Moore comes up to our truck and he's like, you let them take Michele.

Mike Arnold: He's mad at me.

Lissa Casey: Yeah. He got mad. He's like, you let them take Michele. Where are they taking her?

Mike Arnold: He's a former Army Ranger. He's like, what have you done?

Lissa Casey: We're like, we don't know.

Mike Arnold: I was like, I don't know.

Lissa Casey: I look at Mike and then what do we do? Mike says, "I guess we're gonna go to the Burns airport." So, Michele is speeding off in the Kia, she's just been whisked away by FBI agents. That was not the plan. So, we're not really sure what's happening. So, we decide to go to the Burns municipal Airport. Because, we don't really know where to go, because they won't let us near the Refuge and they say you can't go any further.

Mike Arnold: The FBI actually tell us not to follow them. So, I'm like yeah…We're going to go just real fast behind the Kia. So, we jump behind the Kia. We know we're going to the airport because that's where the fortress was for the FBI.

Lissa Casey: And we knew that they were going to stage and get Michele and Rev. Graham together before they took them to the Refuge

Mike Arnold: At this point, we've communicated with everybody. Everybody knows the plan. All of the sudden, it was just you and me in the in the truck and we were driving to eastern Oregon, we've never been this far east before.

Lissa Casey: Nope. Well, I had… Back in January.

Mike Arnold: Yes. So, you're familiar with it. Your description of it and a couple photos you brought back, it just didn't do it justice. It was nothing like I pictured. I've seen videos. I've seen stuff on TV and it's just not the same.

Lissa Casey: I think it was the way that you described it, when we were first talking to the press at the beginning of the case. You said when you are explaining, you know ranchers and how ranchers are not our enemy and how you know we have to use the western lands for our food. You said, at one of our press conferences, you know people out east don't understand how big these states really are and how vast this land really is. And it's hard to picture until you're there, until you're driving and at all times you can see so many miles away. It really doesn't do it justice until you see it.

Mike Arnold: You either see a horizon line or mountains, in the far distance, couple of lower outcroppings and this is not central Oregon, where you have a high desert plateau. I mean, it's just the high desert.

Lissa Casey: So, we decide we're going to go to Burns Municipal Airport. We follow and of course they don't allow us onto the staging area.

Mike Arnold: We met a couple of unnamed FBI, presumably FBI, agents.

Lissa Casey: They're decked out.

Mike Arnold: They're in full battle rattle.

(Photo: The welcome wagon at the Burns Airport.)

Lissa Casey: Full battle rattle. So, we just walk up and start chatting with him. Just try to find out what we can find out, hey how you doing? What are you guys doing here? It was such a surreal moment to be standing out at the Burns Municipal Airport when we know that it's locked down and that the FBI has taken it over. I just know I'm casually chatting with a couple FBI agents.

(Photo: Lissa texting Michele while at the Burns Airport.)

Mike Arnold: What did they say to us?

Lissa Casey: I think we're just trying to do small talk and figure out how far we can get. I'm just asking, how's your day going, what are you guys up to? It was surreal and they were clearly just trying to keep us occupied.

Mike Arnold: Then they told us to leave. So we pulled in the parking area. They told us, you guys need to leave, you can't be around here. I'm like, yeah, whatever. We pull back 5 feet onto the shoulder, halfway into the ditch, right?

Lissa Casey: Yep. And, you're still trying to get on the phone with people to let them know what's going on. Finally we weren't getting anywhere. So, you said, "Let's get in the truck."

So, we get in the truck and I said, "Where are we going?"

You looked at me and you were intense about it. You said, "We're going to go as far as they let us go." And you just start speeding off.

I'm like, alright. We're going.

(Photo: Heading to the Narrows.)

So, we ride toward the roadblock and The Narrows and we set up camp there. ["The Narrows" is The Narrow RV Park and Restaurant, located 26 miles south of Burns on Highway 205 adjacent to the Refuge.]

Mike Arnold: We actually pulled to the very front of the others. It is just the weirdest situation.

Lissa Casey: So weird.

Mike Arnold: So, you're going towards the mountains. I don't even know what mountains those are.

Lissa Casey: Are they the Steens?

Mike Arnold: The Steens. Yeah. That might be it. So, you're just driving and then there's this left-hand turn, this little road and turn left on the right is The Narrows.

Lissa Casey: Which is this little restaurant.

Mike Arnold: It's an old community. But, it's not just a restaurant.

Lissa Casey: Yeah. There was an RV park and then right down the road is the Oregon State Police roadblock.

Mike Arnold: We're driving in and there are cars lining on the side of the road.

Lissa Casey: With people dressed up holding protest signs. I remember the two that stuck out to me. This guy was dressed in military gear standing on top of the car just solemnly standing there the whole time. I mean, this is January or February at this point in eastern Oregon, it's cold. There's this family with their little baby there holding the protest sign on the side of the road. Then there is the press.

Mike Arnold: There's tons of press.

Lissa Casey: It is just crowded. So, we pull right up to the front.

Mike Arnold: It's a narrow road, on the left and the right side of the road. It's just packed with cars.

Lissa Casey: Press and protesters.

Mike Arnold: Press and protesters. We just drive down the middle, my goal is to see how far we can get and so we drive and drive and drive and finally an Oregon State police officer jumps on the road. We don't get within... I don't know, would you say hundred feet?

Lissa Casey: Yeah. It was. There's this big lighted sign that read, "Roadblock subject to arrest."

Mark Arnold: And so, we jump out of the car and what we do?

Lissa Casey: Well, the press surrounds you and they want to know why you're there and what's going on. I went around your back. There's a picture out there they keep using of you talking to the press. I'm kind of behind the car texting back because, at this point we're texting our colleagues. We can't get the live feed on reception. So, we're texting Emilia Gardner back at the Arnold Law office and she's telling you and me what's happening out there so that we can figure out our next moves.

Mike Arnold: There's limited cell service. You can't get any Internet. You can't get any streaming audio. So, Emilia is texting us. Basically, a live update of what she's hearing on the live feed.

Lissa Casey: Then, we go back and we convene at The Narrows.

Mike Arnold: I think at this point, don't we ask to speak to somebody in the FBI?

Lissa Casey: No, that was after we got the recording of Ammon.

Mike Arnold: So, we walk up and actually I have to go to the bathroom. I go behind some sagebrush and I take a knee, like rugby style. And this gal from Oregon State Police comes up to me and she's like, yeah we have in-car-video running of you.

Lissa Casey: On all of our cars.

Mike Arnold: On all of our cars… So we can see you. We have a video of you peeing. So, I was like, alright, Well I guess… Nobody wants to see that.

Lissa Casey: So, we go back to The Narrows.

Mike Arnold: We drive.

Lissa Casey: Yeah. We drove. I think John Moore drove us back. We parked your truck.

Mike Arnold: Shelley Shelton's… What's Shelly Shelton's husband's name, Michele?

Michele Fiore: That was Tony. Tony Shelton.

Lissa Casey: Tony Shelton. Yeah. Drove us back. And we start communing at The Narrows. We're trying to reach Ammon, because we finally have cell service, we're trying to reach the office. Now we can reach people. We're trying to figure out what to do and that I remember, we were sort of waiting it out and we hear that something had happened on the live feed. David Fry had said something and I remember, looking at you and Shelley Shelton came over and started conferring with us. I said, "It's time to get a recording of Ammon. It's time to do that now."

Mike Arnold: I think at this point, Rev. Graham, Michele and Mark of the FBI had got three of the final four to exit and all that's left is David Fry. Emilia keeps texting us that he sounds suicidal, you know, that some things are going to go wrong, he may kill himself.

Lissa Casey: And he was saying that. I mean it wasn't something Emilia was inferring. He was suicidal on the live feed, he was saying that he was afraid to go to prison, that this was the day he was going to die. I mean it was pretty clear. Michele and Rev. Graham had got the other three out, but you know, David was holding out because he was scared.

Mike Arnold: So let's back up to Michele. You are in a black SUV and you pull pass the road block. What happens next, Michele?

Michele Fiore: Well, then we spill out from the black SUV and we hopped into the big armored BearCat.

Mike Arnold: This is far away from the road block. This is miles from the roadblock, right? You have to go past the road block; you drive real long ways and I think you take a left or something and then you get to the entrance to the Refuge. Do you even get that close or is it at the staging point?

Michele Fiore: Once we got into the BearCat, we went right up to the Refuge. So in the BearCat we were right up there.

Mike Arnold: Describe a BearCat. What's it look like in the outside and the inside?

Michele Fiore: So the BearCat is what you would typically see in Las Vegas. It is like an armored, bullet proof, bomb proof, militarized vehicle that keep our officers safe from harm when they are basically going into battle with citizens or terrorists. Inside it is this big emptiness, with benches, so we can fit bodies in there. So it was just Franklin Graham and myself, and Mark, the head of the FBI. I have to give kudos to Mark. That guy was calm, cool, collected. He is a great guy.

Mike Arnold: So what happens next? Like how close do you get? What can you see?

Michele Fiore: So we see everything. So we are right on the ridge, we see the tent, I believe we see Sean's truck, the white pickup truck. Actually, it is funny because last night when I, at the court house when I went over to visit with Ammon for a couple of hours and Sean Anderson was waiting for me and I literally got to go get in that truck last night, because I am staying at the Benson and Sean drove to the Benson and we ate at the Benson last night. So I actually drove in that truck last night, so we saw the truck. The fabulous four, they were not in any of the Refuge buildings. They were camping outside. They just didn't want to do anything.

Mike Arnold: Are you on the ridge? Like are you high above them? Are you on the road?

Michele Fiore: I am on the road.

Mike Arnold: Okay. Let me help with some perspective. So you pull into the front entrance of the Refuge. There is basically a hillside that goes down fairly steep, I don't even know if a BearCat could go down it. It would be difficult. It's the high ground there. But it tactically makes it difficult for something to go down something so steep. At the front of the Refuge, there was a trench. It was described to me by folks in military as a tank trap. So there was basically a narrow squeeze point where only a vehicle could go down this one slot and the only other spot they could go off of was either a hillside or the one flat spot with a trench. So there is no way to get down there unless you squeeze through this one point. And then if you are looking at the entrance to the right down the hill are all these buildings, there is a pond right in front of you down the hill and to the left there is a driveway and a large parking area. Far at the left of the very edge of what would be you know, civilization on the Refuge, was a big tent. And at the edge of this tent was another trench that faced down the road. So if you look at the Refuge straight on, there is the driveway and a little pinch spot. There is the first tank trap, there is the hill, but if somebody wanted to invade the Refuge and take out these final four, they can also kick down the fence further down the road and go through some frozen ground that leads up to the final four and the tent. And there is another hill to their right. So they had essentially dug another tank trap, they call 'The Latrine' but it not a latrine. I've jumped into it, it's super deep, I don't know probably 6 feet, 8 feet deep.

Lissa Casey: When you first saw it, you just went, this is not a latrine. This is a trench.

Mike Arnold: It was complete B.S. I mean, I have no military training. I am like this is a tank trap. And so they had employed a defensive tactic of basically digging a trench to prevent a BearCat from invading them in the middle of the night. So they are fairly protected. I mean human beings can easily sneak up on them and get in there but there wasn't going to be any armored vehicles getting very close. You know, you are on the ridge above them and what happens next?

Michele Fiore: So then we basically start talking to them through the loud speaker. So I say hi, it's Michele, I am here, Franklin is here. Then Franklin gets on some of the speakers and he says something...

Lissa Casey: I remember we were still able to hear at times here, I think updates from Emilia, but maybe I listened to the live feed later. So I remember Michele kept saying to them, they are not going to kill you with all these people listening. They are not going to kill you with me and Franklin Graham here. Let us come in and get you out and we will walk out arm in arm. We will walk out together. They are not going to kill you because the world is listening. There are thousands of people that are going to hear. And so you are trying to use the live feed that was still going as a tool to get them to come out and diffuse their fear.

Michele Fiore: So what I may say, another thing that I didn't tell you guys is it's a few minutes, once we started talking to them, they pulled us back, they pulled Franklin and I back and at this time I had to go to the bathroom. I ask the FBI guy, do you have a porta potty? He's like 'No.' Well I got to go and he told me to go pee behind that sign over there. So I said okay. And there was a helicopter right above us. So I go, I chose a little spot. So I go and so I do this and the helicopter was hovering right over me. So I go to Mark and I say, "Mark, please tell your FBI guy like whoever is in that damn helicopter, don't be using my peeing in bushes footage anywhere."

And he says, "That's not FBI; that's the news."

Mike Arnold: How in the world does the news get access to fly over the Refuge?

Michele Fiore: Yeah, when it was supposed to be a no-fly zone, right?

Mike Arnold: That's insane. And so at 10:14am, I am texting Jordan at the FBI, we are at the diner by the blockade. My pickup is closest to the blockage. So I guess at this point you are negotiating or at least giving them some assurances. Like what were you thinking at the time? What is going on in your mind? What are you seeing? What are you hearing? What are you feeling?

Michele Fiore: You know, I am seeing the FBI being calm now because I finally got to meet Mark. And if you recall, Mark was the negotiator on the phone that I actually wanted to reach through the phone and choke his ass myself because he was antagonistic the night before.

Mike Arnold: Yeah, what did he do? What did he do and say the night before?

Michele Fiore: The night before I don't want to get my words crossed, but he was really cold and he was saying, "Come in here; it's warm. We got hot cocoa." I mean he was just taunting them.

Mike Arnold: I haven't listen to live feed because whole experience quite honestly traumatized me a little. I don't want to listen to it. I was very stressed that night and I have just chosen not to listen to it. But what I was told was that he was saying to the final four, "Look, you've been abandoned. No one's coming. The militia doesn't care about you." And it just didn't seem to be a good faith negotiation. I don't know, it's probably a negotiation tactic to make people feel hopeless and alone, but to me, hopeless and alone meant dying alone and being vulnerable to the FBI. This is what they would be thinking.

Lissa Casey: Firefight.

Michele Fiore: Yeah, it wasn't in good faith, I'll tell you that. But then I got there, and Franklin Graham and I were there talking to the last four. The FBI guy present is Mark, that guy who I just wanted to put my hands over his mouth and shut him up the night before, he literally broke down in tears when David Fry came out.

Mike Arnold: Let's back up. Let's kind of go sequentially. So what were you and Franklin Graham doing and saying and what was the FBI doing when there were still four left?

Michele Fiore: Once Franklin Graham and I got there, Franklin Graham and I got the speakers and they let Franklin Graham and I communicate with them.

Mike Arnold: Were they reluctant to let you do that or they were pretty cool about it?

Michele Fiore: No, Mark was very cool. Mark the head of the FBI, that guy is just very cool. I think he is from the East Coast. I was thoroughly impressed with him and he was just great.

Mike Arnold: Yeah, he was great with me on the phone. He actually calmed me down too.

Michele Fiore: Yeah, and so Mark and I talked about working on other situations such as this when there is no true communication between the patriot movement and the federal government, because the patriot, I get the patriot movement. They are tired of the overbearing, lawless, bureau of land management that's basically the agency of terror.

Mike Arnold: And so what's going on on the phone, what is going on on the speaker?

Michele Fiore: So on the speakers. Sean and Sandy want to come out together, holding hands, holding the flag. They were amazing and they came out and as soon as they came out we embraced them. Sandy, I remember, had her hands cuffed in front of her. She picked her hands up, so I was kind of under her hands. So as I was hugging her, she was hugging me back, you know, handcuffed and Jeff Banta had just come out and then it was David Fry.

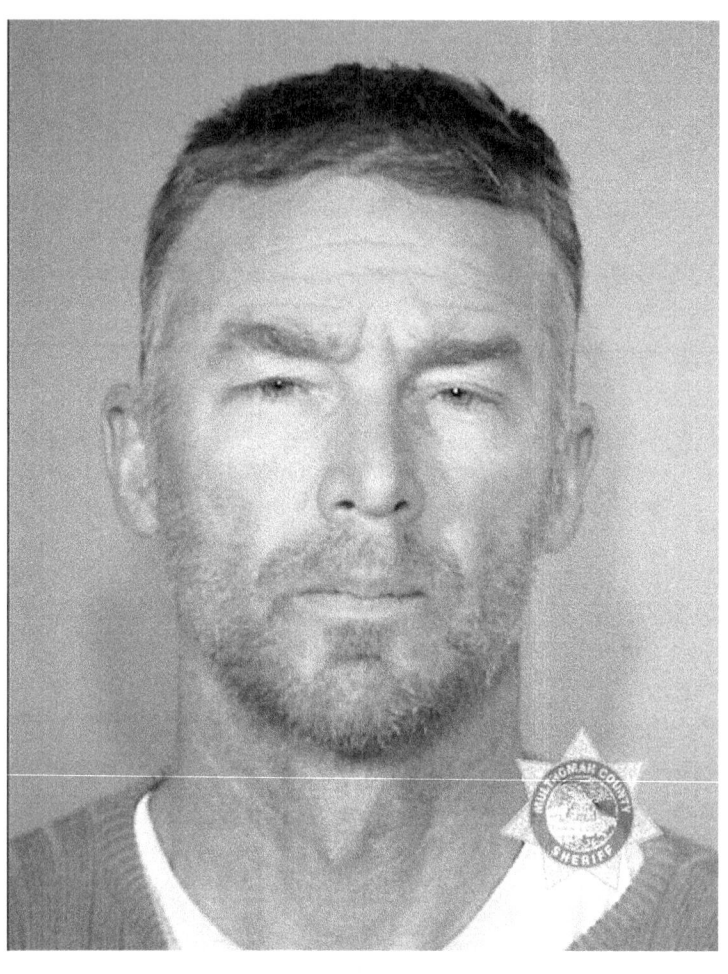

(Photo: Jeff Banta's 2016 mugshot.)

Mike Arnold: So we are back at The Narrows and we got a text message from Emilia that three of them have come out. We were ecstatic. Everybody was excited. And then the tone kind of changed at some point, what happened?

Michele Fiore: So David Fry, he was basically very afraid to go to jail. I don't blame him. David Fry is a very unique young man and he is just beautiful. I mean he is from a lineage of a very decorated military family, from his father's side. And then his mother is this beautiful Asian woman. And so he's got that mix and he has this long beautiful hair and he is a little guy and he is still innocent. He is only 27. And so he is just afraid to go to jail. Who wouldn't be, right?

Mike Arnold: Can you see him? Like what are you looking at? Like what can you see out the window of the BearCat?

Michele Fiore: We are not at the window. We are literally standing at the top of the ridge with the other three and I can see David coming out of the tent and he's got a hoodie on and he puts the hoodie over his head and he goes in the tent, he comes back out, he goes back in and this is at the time when you guys, I have again, my little superheroes, you just found out what was going on. I want you to take this over because Mike calls Ammon in jail and gets a 95 second clip. And if you go through that, I am going to go back through security because this is vital and no one is giving Ammon credit for this. Because this is Ammon's moment.

Lissa Casey: So I remember we went back and tried to find a quiet place to call Ammon at The Narrows and we are like back in the storage room of the rest room.

Mike Arnold: We are actually in the car with, was it Tony? We are in the SUV and then at some point we wanted to get Ammon on the phone. We couldn't do it. So I remember jumping out of the...

Lissa Casey: We went back to The Narrows.

Mike Arnold: Yeah, I remember sprinting in my suit, I had a three piece suite on and my dress shoes. I remember sprinting 300 meters back to the Refuge because I am hearing that David Fry is going to kill himself.

Lissa Casey: And just to be clear, you had flat dress shoes and I was sprinting you in heels. So I sprinted around 300 meters in my heels that day back to The Narrows, just trying to get Ammon on the phone.

Mike Arnold: Well, I didn't see you do that because I can run faster in flats.

Lissa Casey: So we get back there, I remember looking at the storage closet of The Narrows with their food.

Mike Arnold: Right. W go back there because it was better cell reception there.

Lissa Casey: And there were reporters.

Mike Arnold: And we needed lots of privacy to talk to our client.

Lissa Casey: Yes, so we go back and we get Ammon on the phone and we get him to make a statement specifically to David.

Mike Arnold: So we tell him what the goals are and he doesn't know because he is like, he is locked up in jail. So we have to brief him on this. It is overwhelming for him. He just learned that his dad was arrested. This is a very emotional day for Ammon. But the thing is I think that your phone died at this point. We only had one phone and we are on the phone with Ammon there and we don't have the ability to record. So we go and commandeer a cellphone, I don't know if it was Shelby Shelton's or whose it was, but we commandeer our....

Lissa Casey: It was Shelly's attorney's.

Mike Arnold: We commandeer a cellphone and we put it up to the other phone on speaker and we record this statement from Amon.

Lissa Casey: And I remember after we get that statement, I have the statement in my hand and I have Ammon on the phone and I am giving him a play by play of what I am doing and you know, as Michele said, credit should be given to Ammon. There are picture of me going up to the road block and coming back. I am not talking to the press at this point and I am doing that because Ammon's saying, just pass the press, just get the statement there. And he doesn't want me to talk to them, he is not doing this for anybody but David Fry at this point. He is instructing me to walk past the press and I remember a reporter yelled at me, do you have a comment? I said, no comment. I said to Ammon, I am walking and [the reporter] says, "This is the biggest story in the state. You don't have anything to say to us?"

I say, "Nope," and I keep walking. And I remember, it is an image that is burned into my brain. I have the statement and I went up to the road block and they see me running up to them in heels, and in unison, three Oregon State troopers open their driver side doors and they stand up and they are looking at me like, they are going to tackle me if I keep going and I am like, I am running up to you in heels. I have a cellphone like clearly I am not doing anything except trying to get information. So I get up there and I say, I have a statement from Ammon, it needs to get to David Fry. And he says, well, you know, we can't do that for you right now. And I am like, okay, I can't remember what I said to him, something to the effect of, if this doesn't get to them, this is on you. This is not on me because I need this to get to them. So we go back to Tony Shelton's car and I remember OSP brings us the business card for the public information officer of the Harney County Sheriff's department or something. And Mike says, "Yeah, that's okay. I have the FBI on my cellphone. We will just go back to The Narrows."

(Photo: David Fry's 2016 mugshot at the Multnomah County Jail)

Mike Arnold: I mean, I was floored. The Oregon State Police did nothing to facilitate us getting the message to the FBI. I mean nothing...

Michele Fiore: But how did you get it to the FBI? Mike got it and Mark played it over to the loud speaker.

Mike Arnold: Well, what happened was, I am trying to text it and it won't send to anybody. It keeps bouncing back. It is only 96 seconds long. It was not a really big file. So I am trying to figure out how to do it. So I keep just walking around and go into a different spots to try to find reception. So ultimately I am able to text this file to I believe Mark or Jordan, one of them it works. I tried to send it to you several times, Michele, it didn't work. And so ultimately they get it and how did you learn about it?

Michele Fiore: So Mark which is the head of the FBI, he gets it and I can't give him enough kudos. He was just an amazing person and he gets it to the negotiator in the BearCat closest, like literally maybe twenty-thirty from somewhere the camp was and he puts it on the bullhorn or whatever you call that speaker system.

AMMON BUNDY MESSAGE: *David, this is Ammon Bundy. I want you to know that there is a future out here. That you have a future. You've been valiant in your stand for your country and for your rights. Your actions here really matter, that we love you and yeah, things will not be easy at first but we know that the American people are going to stand with us. They are going to stand for your rights, for my rights and we are going to get this thing straightened out. And you need to be part of this even though it might be difficult for you for a few weeks, but we want you to be part of this. We know you have been valiant in your stand and we ask you, do not take your life, and come here and let's work this together and we know the American people are going to stand and make this right. You are part of that. So please come out of there and let us work this out. And I love you very much. Thank you for your valiant efforts...because you love your neighbor, and because you love this land and you love freedom. And go through this with us. Thank you.*

Mike Arnold: So yeah, so what happened when that was played?

Michele Fiore: So then as soon as that was played, Fry says, okay, I need to hear a hallelujah, give me a hallelujah. We weren't understanding. He just wanted Mark, the negotiator, to say hallelujah. So finally, Mark gets it and he says hallelujah, hallelujah, hallelujah. David, you know, comes running out and obeys all the commands and stuff. So at the beginning I was going to kind of give Mark some of Michele's lingo from the night before, you know, I was kind of pissed off from the night before and so we get David and we embrace David and we spent time praying. And by the way, Sean and Sandy talked to David and Jeff Banta talked to David and basically, we can't do this without the last one and we were the fabulous four, so there were many, many people that were talking to David and when he heard Ammon's message, it was, I think that was really key for him coming out. And so when we got to spend time to hug and pray with everyone with Franklin and I, then we got to go up to Mark and as I am walking towards Mark, the negotiator, he is looking at me, I mean I am looking at him and he just breaks down, crying. How can I yell at this FBI negotiator? So I just give him a big hug and thank him because no one got killed. And so as angry as I was with him the night before, his tears made him more of a human and totally humanized him about the stress he was going through and the no sleeping and all that stuff. So it was definitely a telling moment to where our opinions evolved into. People are people and we just have to make sure that we humanize everyone.

(Photo: Sandy and Sean Anderson's mugshots in 2016.)

(Photo: Sandy and Sean Anderson outside the federal
courthouse in Portland during the 2016 trial.)

Lissa Casey: We were getting updates about this via text still
from Emilia back at the office and we get a message that David
Fry has come out and that everybody is safe. And what we heard
from Emilia was, I mean because we were just getting bits and
pieces of this from Michele, so I remember walking back up to
the road block and getting into Mike's truck because we realize it
is time to you know, kind of decompress and some cameras got
in my face and the journalist said, what happened and I said that
he asked for a cigarette and a cookie and for everybody to
say hallelujah, because those were the three pieces of information
we had and then I said: "everybody is safe" and I shut the door

of the truck and we drove off. And that was a pretty surreal moment, I mean that's what we heard about how it ended. So we went back to The Narrows and we waited for you and Rev. Graham to come back.

Mike Arnold: So there was this big black SUV and Michele and Rev. Graham popped up. And who was driving that SUV? Was that Mark?

Michele Fiore: That was Mark.

Mike Arnold: Okay. So I finally got to meet Mark and you know, you give a big farewell hug to the Reverend and you hold a little press conference. Everyone decompresses. We eat. I think I had was this big chicken fried steak dinner, what was the gal's name at The Narrows? She was wonderful.

(Photo: Michele and the reverend embrace at the Narrows.)

Michele Fiore: I had the milkshake at the Narrows. They are famous for those milk shakes.

Mike Arnold: I remember everyone was so nice there.

Lissa Casey: It was so nice.

Mike Arnold: So actually, I remember while we were waiting. We had lots of time to kill. So what were we doing when we were not running around being crazy?

Michele Fiore: And being superheroes. You guys, I have so many photos of you guys running off that dirt road and as I saw them all in the paper, I am thinking those are my superheroes. You guys were amazing.

Mike Arnold: What were we doing?

Lissa Casey: We were trying to get cell reception; we were trying to call Ammon.

Mike Arnold: But that was down time.

Lissa Casey: We were just eating good food. We were hanging, a lot of the politicians were there at The Narrows kind of waiting and hoping. There was media there and...

Mike Arnold: I remember that one point, there was somebody that got a car wreck with a deer. What happened then?

Lissa Casey: I think it was a Washington Post reporter, right?

Mike Arnold: Yeah.

Lissa Casey: Some young woman comes in and she pulls up her car and the front of it is all messed up and so she says, "I'm from the Washington Post. I was driving out here to cover this and I hit a deer." And so Mike decides, because this is a thing...

Mike Arnold: She asked for a tow truck, and she wanted somebody to get her car and fix it.

Lissa Casey: And you were like, no, I am just going to lay my suit jacket in this pot really quick, get some bailing twine from my pickup truck and then fix your car in the parking lot of the Narrows because that's just what Mike does.

Michele Fiore: We got a snap of that too. That was another heroic moment.

Mike Arnold: We tried to tell her, "You are in the middle of nowhere. There is nothing open.

She said, "I need to drive back to Idaho."

"Well, you are not going to be able to do that dragging your bumper and this light."

So I went to Linda Gainer, the owner of the Narrows, and said, "Do you have any duct tape?" Any farmer knows, any rancher knows, you can fix anything with duct tape.

(Photo: Mike with the owner of the Narrows, Linda Gainer.)

Michele Fiore: I think it is a man thing, Mike. You guys use duct tape to fix everything. That's a man thing.

Mike Arnold: You actually need take the next step. Duct tape alone doesn't fix everything. As every farmer knows, it's duct tape plus bailing twine. So I grabbed a big handful of bailing twine and I had a pocket knife in my pocket. I laid my jacket down underneath the front end of her car and man it smelled so bad. There was deer blood and fur, and man, eastern Oregon mule deer, they stink. So I am getting my fingers all gummed up by little bits of this beautiful mule deer that she apparently hit on some open road around the sage brush. With a little bit of elbow grease we were able to fix this thing and send her on our way. And that's essentially what we did. We just kind of hung out and waited, because it was just hard to describe what it was like to not have any information. We are so used to instant information nowadays that when you are in the dark in the middle of nowhere and you are not getting a live stream or a live update, you don't know what it is going on. And in hindsight we know all these facts, we know the players. But at the time, it was really stressful.

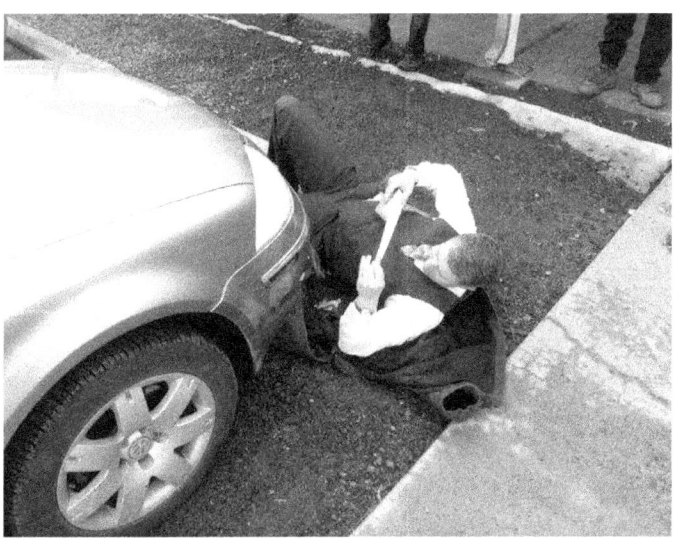

(Photo: Mike at the Narrows killing time waiting
for Michele to return.)

Lissa Casey: We were trying to make all these decisions on limited information, from just the updates that were getting and you know, lives were on the line and it's just not a situation you find yourself in every day as two lawyers in the middle of eastern Oregon waiting out an FBI negotiation with an assembly woman and a reverend in a bearcat and trying to get reception running for up to an OSP road block, past cameras and protestors. I mean the whole thing was just completely surreal.

(Photo: Reverend Graham on the left with FBI and Michele after they dropped Michele off at the Narrows parking lot minutes after the end of the Oregon Standoff.)

Michele Fiore: The funny thing is that right now we are going through in Nevada the Bunkerville trial, and the FBI has posed as a filmmaker, in the Bunkerville standoff.

Mike Arnold: Yeah, it was Long Bow Productions.

Michele Fiore: Long Bow Productions, yeah. What most don't know is they lied to me, as an elected official. I literally went into their trailer. It was beautiful by the way, probably at least a million-dollar trailer, taxpayer dollars spent on this trailer.

Lissa Casey: Mike says they print the money. So it is not surprising that the trailer was nice.

Michele Fiore: So yeah, the trailer was beautiful, all equipped. The last thing was this documentary and they did it well; I just saw about fifteen minutes of it. And what that told me is the narrative that they showed me was totally on the side of what happened against the BLM. So what they were doing was that they were collecting enough footage to make a whole different narrative to suit their purposes. And first of all when you lie to an elected official, it is not...so, Mike, you and I have to talk. I am just not okay with that. I am not okay with another unelected agency trying to entrap an elected official.

Mike Arnold: This whole situation was outside of our realm of experience. You were running off of common sense and I was running off of, I don't know what. The FBI was helping. Everybody was helping one another. I think that this was a group of effort of a bunch of people that just cared about the outcome being safe.

Lissa Casey: And lives being preserved.

Mike Arnold: It was an interesting life experience. So I appreciate you taking the time to share that with us Michele. I know you have to testify later today. I assume Ammon Bundy is testifying right now.

Michele Fiore: Yeah, he is on the stand now. Or maybe they just broke, people are coming out.

Mike Arnold: Thanks for coming, Michele.

Lissa Casey: It was nice to talk to you, Michele.

Michele Fiore: Hey, I love you guys.

Afterword

Ammon Bundy testified at the trial for the defense for three days with his trial attorney Marcus Mumford of Idaho guiding him through his direct examination. The government cross-examined him for only 15 minutes, symbolizing their arrogant belief that Ammon's words weren't even worth the jury's time. Two words, however, were worth the jury's time: "Not guilty"...on all counts...for all defendants.

Ammon and the protesters at his trial were acquitted while the remaining Oregon protesters are awaiting their Oregon federal trial. Ammon and his brother Ryan Bundy were thereafter transported to Nevada to stand trial for the 2014 Bunkerville Standoff. And their story continues...

(Photo: Lissa and Michele taking a break to enjoy the review on the way back to Portland to meet with Ammon and then hold a press conference with elected officials.)

Photo: Mike and Michele on the way back to Portland).

BONUS True Crime Story Book Excerpt: *Finishing Machine* (Part 1)

Prologue: Predator or Prey?

The evening was cool and a haze hung low over a dark, rural road where only a truck's headlights provided illumination. It was January in Springfield, Oregon, so a low fog was not unexpected. But as the evening deepened, the clouds suddenly gave way to a brief, un-forecasted downpour.

One man, trained as a Marine sniper, found himself standing alone. Moments before, he and another man – a stranger – had been in a confrontation. Then came the rain. And now there was only a lingering mist, backlit by the headlights.

He had been trained by the military for exactly this: a coolly evaluated threat, followed by a split-second decision to take action. But he wasn't on the gun range, not tonight. He hadn't calculated his move through the lens of a scope, and he hadn't picked off his target from a safe and detached distance. There were no instructions from afar. This was different. It was up close and personal. The cloudburst had not been rain, and the mist was not made up of water. It was bits of blood, brain, skin and skull.

The shooter lowered his gun, and raised his cell phone to his ear. He needed an ambulance. A man lay shattered on the pavement, his life ebbing away as cars continued to flow past the scene. All around, an audience of dark homes, fences and trees stood as silent witnesses to what had occurred. A woman, having left the safety of her vehicle to investigate the sounds she had heard, screamed at the sight of the long black gun and the violence it had wrought.

Was there any doubt who was the predator, and who was the prey?

(Photo: Dramatization of the final moments.)

Chapter 1: A Potential Case?

I was at home on my small farm outside Creswell, Oregon, on the night of the shooting. Having put my four-year-old daughter to sleep by reading Dr. Seuss' "The Pale Green Pants" a couple of times front to back, I had returned to the living room to relax. The house was quiet, the lights dimmed. The wood stove was stoked with Douglas fir rounds that I had bucked from a fallen tree from the wooded part of our property the previous year. While enjoying the warmth of the fire, I alternated between reading a case file and online news stories. I noticed a story of gun violence pop up online. Curious, I began reviewing the sparse but gripping details on the small screen of my iPhone.

My name is Mike Arnold and I am a criminal defense attorney who specializes in complex cases. I am the managing partner of an eight-attorney firm located in Eugene, Oregon, almost two hours south of Portland ... and just across the Willamette River from Springfield, where the shooting I was reading about had occurred.

The criminal defense section of my firm was built on the bread and butter of low-level crime, cases involving domestic violence, driving under the influence, sexual assault, etc. I had consulted on several murder cases, but never defended one on my own. This largely owed to the fact that violent crime isn't that common in this part of the Willamette Valley. Any gun crime that occurs catches people's attention in a big way, and that is especially true for members of the local bar. Defense attorneys like me know that we'll receive an inquiry call on at least half of the cases that our community considers "high profile." That's why I pay close attention to crimes when they are reported. It helps me be ready when someone in trouble (or the family member) makes that initial phone call.

On their websites, the local newspaper and all three television stations provided breaking details of the Springfield shooting: there had been a motor-vehicle collision, the parties had argued, an assault rifle had been brandished, and an unnamed man was shot dead. Road rage, police speculated.

Road rage by whom?

While most people confronted with these preliminary details would assume that the shooter was the hothead, it was instinctive for me to consider the opposite possibility, that the decedent himself was the bad actor. That's just how defense attorneys are; we tend to take a 360-degree view of every set of facts we encounter. We know from experience that things are not always as they seem.

After refreshing the screen a few times and checking some other news outlets for the additional details I was hungry for, I found myself going into criminal defense mode. In my head I worked through the various scenarios by which a roadside shooting could be considered legally justifiable, mentally plotting out how I would handle each one in a pleading or a courtroom argument. Thinking three steps ahead – or 30 – is an occupational hazard in my business. But I knew that most of my speculation would be fruitless until more was known about the incident. For the man with the gun, the facts, when established, would make the difference between a self-defense-based exoneration on all charges, or life in prison on a murder conviction.

Toggling between the online briefs, I found myself wondering how badly the vehicles had been damaged, because it would tell me something about the speed of the vehicles at impact. But the photos and videos that had been posted were too dark to tell me anything, and it frustrated me. Don't news photographers and TV cameramen carry spotlights?

More questions popped to mind. How far was the decedent from the crash when he was shot? Did the shooter fire from inside his vehicle, or from the road? I noticed that one TV reporter had captured footage showing a small canopy erected over what was presumably the dead man's body.

C'mon, somebody give me an estimate of distance! Report on something other than what the police tell you!

My curiosity, you should know, was not entirely professional. As a concealed firearm carrier, I am always interested in the circumstances of shooting deaths. I try to put myself in the shoes of both sides like a jury does, trying to figure out what happened and how it could have ended differently. I want to understand the details so I can learn from them, and not just as an attorney. I don't want to be the victim of a shooting, and I don't want to shoot anything other than blacktail deer and other four-legged prey. The two-legged type? Only in the pixelated video games of my youth.

Courtesy of a subsequent news update, I learned that the shooter was claiming self-defense and had been released after questioning. Police said that charges, if any, would be lodged after an investigation was complete.

This didn't surprise me. That's how these cases usually go at the beginning. But now the story had me completely hooked.

This was a case I could personally relate to and feel morally confident in defending. My work as an attorney had made me an ardent believer in, and strong advocate of, the Second Amendment to the Constitution. As an American citizen, I have the right to bear arms, and a right to use them to defend myself and my family. As the holder of a concealed carry permit, I often have a handgun tucked under my shirt or suit jacket. I don't enjoy carrying a firearm; in fact, I'm more comfortable leaving it at home. But I see my gun as a necessary tool for the job of living. I'd rather have it and not need it, than need it and not have it.

To me, a gun is not much different than an ax or a pen knife or anything else I use to complete my work around the farm. But there is an important distinction. If I forget to carry a knife to break open the hay bales to feed the livestock, I might have to walk back to the shop to retrieve it (or I might use the ax, if it's nearby, to break the bailing twine). But delay and improvisation are all but impossible when you're in a situation that requires a firearm. What are you going to do, say "Just a minute, I'll be right back," and turn your back on the threat to go get a gun? Of course not. To me, carrying a firearm is like carrying insurance. Maybe you'll never use it, but it's there just in case. As the saying goes, "I carry a gun because a cop is too heavy."

One of the reasons I carry a weapon owes to the particulars of our law practice. My wife and law partner, Jacy, is an excellent divorce lawyer who specializes in complex, high-asset (read: high-stress) cases. Violent behavior and threats go with the territory. I keep a shotgun in the office "just in case." I also carry on my person, and my attorneys and staff are authorized to do the same. Each of us has taken time to plan how to respond and escape in the event of an active-shooter scenario.

Thankfully, I have only had to "use" my firearm twice, and the situations were remarkably similar. On both occasions, domestic-violence victims who were getting restraining orders with the help of our law firm were tailed by their abusers to their appointments with us. Both times the guys aggressively entered the office and angrily demanded to see their wives, terrifying my receptionist. Both times these abusers failed to take no for an answer and threatened to search the office for "their" women. When I appeared and politely asked these men to leave, both times I saw their eyes stray to the Glock 21 visible on my right hip. I don't know if their true intent was violent or if they just wanted to scare our clients (who were well within earshot of both confrontations and were indeed frightened). But I do know that the men quickly apologized for any inconvenience and left. Maybe it was the sight of me, a 220-pound, 6-foot-plus guy…or maybe it was the silent presence of a device made by Gaston Glock.

It shouldn't be surprising then, that I believe the right to bear firearms goes hand in hand with a person's natural right to self-defense. If the shooting I was now learning about online was going to hinge on whether the shooter felt his life was threatened, then I fairly salivated to be part of his defense. The right to use lethal force in response to a threat is a very complicated legal concept, one that offers lawyers plenty of room to plan, argue and maneuver.

The right to self-defense isn't found in the U.S. Constitution. It's an innate right that is a creature of statute, so it varies from state to state. In Oregon, people have the right to use the degree of force they reasonably believe is necessary to stop or prevent the imminent unlawful force of another. When talking to jurors or clients about the right to use force in self-defense, I'm often asked how someone can know when a shot or punch is justified. My answer: If you have time to consider what the police or jury would think if you pulled the trigger or threw the punch, then the threat probably isn't imminent and there's time to remove yourself from the situation. But if you are too preoccupied with surviving the next few seconds to consider the consequences of your actions, that's a different story. You may be found to be legally authorized to defend yourself. That is, unless you're the unfortunate "unreasonable" person who "overreacted" in the eyes of a jury. But it's better to be judged by 12 than carried by six, they say, and that's another phrase I appreciate.

Eventually one of the media sources I was following identified the shooter as 34-year-old Gerald Strebendt, the owner of Northwest Training Center, a mixed martial arts gym in Springfield.

Wait a second. Isn't that where Adam trains?

Adam Shelton, a young associate attorney with our firm, had begun training at Northwest Training Center after relocating from Portland. Not only had he told me about it, I saw the evidence to prove it. Adam sometimes came into the office looking like he had crashed his motorcycle: bruised everywhere and sometimes missing some skin on his legs, arms, elbows or face. Damaging workouts aside, Adam had never failed to speak highly of his training, his gym mates, and yes, his coach. Now I stood looking out an east window at a shadowy stand of oak trees, wondering if Adam had heard yet that his martial arts coach was the shooter. It also made me wonder if Adam's association with the shooter could increase the odds that we would receive a call requesting legal advice. While lots of cases cross our desks, as I've said, the majority of my clients have always come through personal connections with past or present clients, friends, or colleagues.

This put a new and interesting slant on my nighttime news reading. Might this crime and Adam's association with the shooter give me my first real murder case to defend? The experience would greatly enhance my own skills. But the benefits of defending a case such as this would extend beyond me to the associates working for me, up-and-coming young lawyers who were doing criminal defense, family law, and other civil cases. This case could benefit the firm and everyone in it. And, undoubtedly, it would give me the chance to participate in a community discussion about an issue I cared a lot about: the constitutional right to bear arms. Hell, even if the case got nowhere near me or my firm, it was going to be fascinating. For legal voyeurs like me and my associates, just being in the same county with the case was going to be a learning experience.

(Photo: Adam Shelton with Brazilian Ju-Jitsu blue belt in hand and Coach Gerald beside him. 08/09/2013)

Since 2001, when I became a lawyer, the complexity of the criminal defense cases I took on increased pretty slowly – until the last few years. In 2011, I helped get a false rape charge against an Oregon State University student dismissed just days before trial. In the summer of 2013, I successfully defended a first-degree manslaughter charge lodged against my client, who was acquitted in the motorcycle wreck death of his girlfriend. In recent months, I had been very busy with some cases that were significant for a firm our size – a trade secrets case involving the outdoor clothier Columbia Sportswear, a breach-of-contract lawsuit against FedEx, and various criminal cases from around the state.

Could 2014 be the year I would get to apply my practice philosophy to a murder case? Given my age (37), experience, and the short tenure of our firm, it would be a coup to land such a case, given the number of high-quality and experienced criminal defense lawyers in Oregon who would also make anyone's short list.

It wasn't long before the social media comments started rolling in online. Many commenters claimed to have personal knowledge of the Springfield shooting. One asserted that one car rammed the other. Another said that one of the men had been chased from his vehicle by a gun-wielding maniac before he was killed. Others swore that the dead man had been pulled from his vehicle and shot in the back of his head while kneeling in the street. They proclaimed, practically in unison, that the killing was not justified. Some said that Gerald should be executed, just as he had executed his victim. The whole story struck me as sad – horrible, really – and legally messy.

The next wave of incoming information pushed my already strong interest in the case up several more notches, as people began buzzing about the background of the killer. Gerald Strebendt, it turned out, was a minor martial arts celebrity on the national/international scene. He fought at a major Ultimate Fighting Championship (UFC) event more than a decade earlier. He volunteered to coach the University of Oregon's Jiu-Jitsu team, which traveled all over the Northwest to compete. He trained several successful amateur and professional fighters. His mixed martial arts gym seemed to have been built on his two minutes and 45 seconds of UFC fame, his years of competitive professional fighting and training of fighters, and some connections to MMA celebrity Eddie Bravo.

Interestingly, when I googled Gerald Strebendt's name, I found some evidence of local civic involvement to balance the man's profile. He had been a part of the Community Development Advocacy Committee for the City of Springfield. The committee included six at-large community representatives – including Gerald – and had advised the council on housing and community development matters. Still, it took only a look back at the comments below the online articles to see that if I got this case, I'd have my work cut out for me. Posts had begun appearing from people who claimed that Gerald was hot-tempered and had a history of driving aggressively. I continued scouring the internet, knowing that if Adam's connection to the shooter resulted in a consultation, I was going to have to know more about this incident than even Gerald did.

It took an "Are you coming to bed soon?" from my wife to bring me back to some semblance of practicality. My practice was thriving, but I had been struggling for some time with how to balance my work with family life. I had recently set a personal goal to slow down a bit, help more at home, get more done around the farm, and take a more consistent approach to management of the office. I could already tell that those resolutions were in some jeopardy, just judging by how quickly and completely this case caught my attention.

I forced myself back to task – preparing for an existing client's hearing on a 50-plus count indictment. Whenever my thoughts strayed back to this new potential case, I told myself that even if this shooter decided to call Arnold Law, neither I nor the firm were really in a good position to take it on. I was really, really busy and didn't need a new case.

What's more, my right-hand senior associate attorney, Emilia Gardner, had just delivered her second baby. That left the firm seriously short-handed, because if I'm the firm's field marshal, its ideas guy, Emilia is our logistics general, the one who pulls together the troops and gathers the supplies to make things happen. She often gives me a sour look when I crash into her office with some new and overly ambitious plan of action, but if it's in the realm of possibility, Emilia is the one who will make it happen. I knew that if this case did come through the door, it would be nearly impossible to take it on without her as my second chair.

I couldn't resist. I set down my case file and sent a quick text to Emilia, including a link to one of the news stories on the shooting. She'd probably be up with the baby, I figured. Then I emphasized the first text by sending a follow-up: "New case?" Then, not getting an immediate response, I began trying to wrap up my work to get to bed.

Emilia responded within the hour. "Looks bad for shooter," she said. "Brother says he knows him. Sounds guilty. Near my mom's place."

Emilia's mother, Lupe, lived south of Springfield on a country road. "How far away does your mom live?" I wrote.

"About half a mile. It's on the new road that punched the highway through. Used to be a field."

"Could your mom have seen or heard anything?"

"Nah, she's on the other side of the hill."

Then I posed the important question. "Could we handle it?"

"Who is we?" she responded quickly and brusquely. "This baby is my current job. You are on your own."

I had to laugh. If we landed the case, I knew I could talk her into working on it, maybe luring her back to the excitement of a big case with some flexible working hours. But I responded: "We'll talk more tomorrow, when you are more sleep-deprived and malleable."

I knew that Emilia was possible to convince because I had done it before. That big trade-secrets case, the one involving Columbia Sportswear, landed in my lap not long after her first child was born. I was working every minute of the day and sleeping on the floor in my office some nights, really struggling to get up to speed on the hundreds of thousands of pages of documents. Emilia took pity on me, bringing her newborn son to the office to help out until the new case was under control. By that time, however, little Jacob had grown very comfortable with nursing and sleeping in his mama's arms while she reviewed discovery or drafted pleadings. Emilia ended up staying on the case, and Jacob came to work with her until he learned to walk.

(Photo: A very pregnant Emilia with Jacob in hand a few months earlier.)

I hope he calls, I thought. Then I went to bed.

Day dawned surprisingly quickly. I cut short my usual farm chores to get in my truck and drive into town earlier than usual. I wanted to touch base with Adam, my associate. Did he know yet that the guy he trains with was involved in a road-rage shooting?

Adam had indeed heard the news. Fellow martial arts students had spread the word, asserting that Gerald Strebendt was innocent of any crime, and that the incident had left him distraught.

"Reach out to him, be a friend," I suggested to Adam. "Make sure he doesn't talk to the police except to say, 'I want a lawyer.' And tell him not to tell his version of what happened to anybody, not even his friends or family."

By then I knew that Gerald Strebendt was in a load of trouble. The morning's newspaper had identified the shooting victim as an unarmed man in his fifties, significantly older than Gerald, and that Gerald had shot him at close range. Whether it was going to be our firm or somebody else's, this guy needed legal representation in a hurry. I was especially concerned that he not submit to police questioning or interrogation without the presence of counsel because, generally, law enforcement investigators are looking for evidence of guilt, not innocence. They are case-provers, not truth-seekers. I didn't know if Gerald was guilty or innocent, but I have seen clients make their cases much, much worse by talking to law enforcement.

Nor did I want a man in Gerald's position to tell his story to anyone else outside of law enforcement. The inevitable stress-induced glitches in his memory would only hinder his case if the stories he told were inconsistent. Should a friend be subpoenaed to testify, the discrepancies alone could be enough to convict him.

To me, though, it wasn't just a matter of protecting the man's rights and preparing for a potential trial. I also knew from my extensive research into police shootings that when someone takes a life, there's a need for quick psychological and emotional intervention to prevent the development of post-traumatic stress disorder. A good lawyer would assist Gerald in finding that help.

After listening to me ramble on about some of this, Adam raised an ethical concern, and it was an appropriate one. He had only been practicing law for a couple of years, and he worried that contacting his Jiu-Jitsu teacher would represent a violation of Oregon's Rules of Professional Conduct prohibiting the solicitation of clients.

I felt confident, based on my ethics consultations over the years, that Adam could call Gerald to offer some basic and free legal advice. The state actually encouraged it as a matter of public policy. Still, I suggested that Adam review the Oregon RPC for himself. Then he could decide whether his relationship with Gerald – whom he considered a friend – would qualify as an exception to the rule.

It was after noon when Adam flagged me down in the hall. "I tried calling Gerald, but it went straight to voicemail."

"Damn. Oh well. His phone was probably seized as evidence. That's not a good sign for him."

Adam continued. "I sent him a message on Facebook with my cell and work numbers, though. I'll let you know if he calls."

At the end of the day, as I was headed out the door to meet my family for supper, Adam caught me again. "I talked to Gerald," he said.

I stopped and put down my briefcase to give Adam my full attention. "What did he say?"

"He was glad I reached out to him. He doesn't have a phone. As you suspected, SPD took his cell last night."

The phone was probably tucked away in an evidence locker, I knew, either dead by now or buzzing continually.

"How's he doing? Is he okay?"

"Not really. He's pretty freaked out, and he has a lot of questions."

"Did you help him out?"

"I talked to him a little about his rights."

"Just tell me you told him to shut up and not talk to anyone."

"Yeah, of course, and he agreed. He says he's been getting a lot of crazies sending him messages on Facebook about how he's going to jail for the rest of his life. Death threats, too. He had to shut down his account. He asked if you'd meet with him."

"Did you tell him I would?"

"Absolutely. He was relieved to hear it."

"So when's he coming in?"

"Tomorrow, mid-morning. His fiancée, Kristin, is going to bring him."

I got out my phone to check my morning.

Adam waved away my phone. "Don't worry, I already talked to Meagan. She says your calendar's clear."

Together Adam and I walked out the doors of our fourth-floor office onto the open-air landing overlooking the parking lot. I could see the tops of the maple and magnolia trees in the U-shaped courtyard below, flanked by the 1960s brick facade of the Hult Plaza building that Arnold Law calls home. We stopped to talk more, leaning on the aluminum railing of the balcony, which is several inches too low by modern building standards. Adam joined me in surveying the surroundings. With both of us standing at nearly 6'2", the railing touched our thighs just below the tipping point of our centers of gravity. I turned away to look at the gloomy winter skyline to the west and asked, "Do you think Gerald had it in him to kill a guy for no good reason?"

Adam pondered a moment. "Gerald's a good man. But he's complicated. He's been through a lot in his life." Then he chuckled drily. "You should hear some of the stories he tells."

"Well, if he's charged, we will likely be reading those stories, either in police reports or the newspaper. I look forward to meeting him tomorrow." With that, the two of us went downstairs and in opposite directions to our cars.

(Photo: Author Mike Arnold doing morning farm chores
with Honey and Tin-Tin.)

Chapter 2: A Meeting, a Handshake, a Client

The Gerald Strebendt I met the next morning in my law office wasn't my idea of what a mixed-martial-arts fighter would look like, much less a road-rage shooter. He was slighter in stature than I would have guessed, and not as bulked-up as I would have thought, either.

As I walked out into our reception area to greet him, Gerald stood up and stuck out his hand. His grip was firm and strong. It was a good handshake. He smiled in a way that was both welcoming and nervous.

"Thanks for meeting with me on such short notice," he said. Although obviously uncomfortable with the situation, he was notably polite and respectful to me, my staff, and his fiancée Kristin Swenson, who had come with him for moral support.

I gathered more impressions of Gerald as I exchanged pleasantries with him and Kristin. First, I was surprised that the man I was sizing up was, at 34, three years younger than me. He seemed older, maybe in the way that sadness or weariness can age a person. Second, when he spoke, I was surprised to hear the tone of his voice. It wasn't gruff or deep. Instead, it was soft, and the pitch was a little higher than mine, maybe on the verge of being considered effeminate.

I remember thinking that MMA and UFC websites must be generous with their stats on fighters, because Gerald didn't look to be 5'9" tall, as his bios claimed. Though supposedly just five inches taller, I felt like a giant towering over him. He also looked to be carrying 40-50 pounds more than the 155-pound fighting weight I'd seen attributed to him online – meaning that I still probably outweighed him by 20-30 pounds. Of course, that didn't mean much. *He can still probably kill me with his bare hands*, I thought.

I then turned my attention to Kristin, Gerald's tall, thirty-ish fiancée. She was very pretty in a strong, athletic-looking way. My hunch – later proven true – was that she had met Gerald while working out in his gym. "I'm going to steal your fella here for a bit," I told her. "I hope you don't mind waiting."

Kristin laughed and dropped into a leather lobby chair, saying, "We figured that. I'm just the chauffeur."

It's standard policy in my office to exclude loved ones or friends when I meet with a client or potential client. There are all kinds of reasons for that, but the big one is protecting the attorney-client privilege. A judge can invalidate the privilege if a third party sits in on a conversation.

I shifted my perspective as Gerald and I walked the short distance to my office. To me, this is a critical moment: I only get one chance to take a juror's point of view of a would-be defendant, and never do I want to squander the opportunity. Does Gerald look reputable and reliable? Clean and careful with his appearance? In his dark-blue jeans and button-down shirt, I would say yes to both questions. His hair was short with the sides clipped close to his head, and there were no obvious tattoos or attention-getting piercings. He looked like any average guy who was beginning to soften with age. You'd hardly notice him if you passed him on the street.

Is this really a professional fighter? A road-rage killer?

I didn't pick up any bad vibes from Gerald at all, and that's saying a lot. All of us at the Arnold Law Firm are good at tuning in on the frequencies of our clients, witnesses, and adverse parties. While most people who come to us are normal people who have just screwed up somehow, we have represented or in some way worked with our fair share of folks with borderline, narcissistic or antisocial personality disorders. Consequently, our "crazy gauge" is always on and usually accurate.

(Photo: Gerald Strebendt appeared to be a "nice guy.")

Gerald didn't seem the "angry man," the "controlling manipulator," or the "likeable charmer" that we often see in violent perpetrators. He just seemed like...*a nice guy.* He came off like a typical small business owner, someone not much different from me – with one big exception, of course. He had recently shot and killed a man.

I motioned for Gerald to sit down in a client chair. "Make yourself comfortable," I said. "I'm going to run down the hall to get some paperwork."

This too, is strategic. I like to "go get paperwork" before beginning a meeting so that people have a chance to sit alone in my office and get comfortable being there. For most, it's their first appointment with an attorney and for many blue collar folks, also their first time in "some suit's office."

Sitting alone, guests can look out a large wall-to-wall window beside my desk to distant trees and hills. Or, they can survey some of the items I've strategically placed in the room to spark small talk. There's a photo of me going over 30-foot Big Brother waterfall on the White Salmon River in Washington, which often prompts the question, "Is that *you?!*" Or maybe they talk about their kids after seeing a photo of my daughter or one of her drawings. My rugby days are over, but years ago you would have found several scrum photos on display. Now only one remains to spark conversation.

I want my visitors to see me as somebody a lot like them, someone who is more than "a suit," because I am. Law degree notwithstanding, I'm just a guy who helps good people find their way past a really bad day in their lives. While the job has its moments of drama, overall it's just a lot of talking to people and staring at a computer screen. Very few of my days look anything like an episode of "Law and Order."

Outside the door of my office, while supposedly "getting papers," I ran through in my head the goals for this conversation. My first priority was to provide Gerald with information that would allow him to protect himself legally as the police investigation went forward. The second priority was to give him some general information about the law as it pertains to self-defense, which I hoped would let him rest a little easier about what lay ahead. Before walking back into the office, I stopped at the printer to pick up the jury instructions for deadly force, so Gerald could take them home and review them.

What is never a goal when first meeting with a client is getting hired. It either happens or it doesn't; we aren't there to sell ourselves. We exist to educate a client in a straightforward, honest manner about his or her rights as an American citizen. Still, experience has shown that this happens to be a pretty effective sales technique. When we answer questions with real knowledge and experience, we almost always prove ourselves to be well-equipped to handle the case.

"Okay then," I said, closing the office door behind me and sitting down in my chair behind the desk. I folded my hands in front of me, hoping that Gerald would open the conversation on his own terms, maybe with some banter, or some comment or question about things he'd seen in my office. But Gerald didn't initiate, so I took the lead with some getting-to-know-you questions. He sat in the green upholstered client chair and answered each question quietly, keeping his head, shoulders, upper body, arms, and hands still. *He's very carefully under control*, I thought.

We started by talking about how he knew my associate, Adam, who like me was a transplant from the Midwest. Then we quickly got to more relevant information. I asked, "How are you doing? Are you getting any sleep?"

"No, sir," he replied. "I haven't eaten or slept much since this happened."

I left it there. I didn't want us to stray into talking about what happened the night of the shooting. I never talk about that on a "first date."

Instead, I went back to rapport-building. I started by asking Gerald where he was from, although I already knew the answer. (It was a first for me to have a client or potential client with his own Wikipedia page.) Gerald confirmed that he was from a rural area outside Coos Bay, Oregon. This led to talking about what it was like to grow up near a coastal cattle ranch owned by his grandfather and two uncles. Plainly, he loved it.

Gerald was surprised to learn that I'm a bit of a rancher, too. This opened the door for me to tell stories of the various ways I've shocked, stabbed, cut, or otherwise broken myself while farming. I have no shortage of these stories, unfortunately. I have grabbed an electric fence while standing in a puddle of water in flip-flops. I have fallen over a fence trying to escape a rushing Angus bull that didn't appreciate my carrying away an abandoned newborn calf and seemed to enjoy the hell out of seeing me end up with splatters of fresh greenish manure on my face. I can tell the story of cleaving off a knuckle while using a handsaw to trim a rafter on a tin roof. I once got stung by dozens of our honey bees, which sent me into anaphylactic shock and required my wife to drag my near-lifeless body into the truck to drive 110 miles per hour to the nearest ER.

Any trial lawyer absolutely must be an above-average story-teller. It's a skill that most of us work to cultivate. After I ran through a couple embarrassing stories starring myself, Gerald began to respond with stories of his own, revealing more and more information about himself. And, I had to admit, the guy was a damn good storyteller in his own right.

I learned that Gerald liked building stuff and making engines sing loud. He loved being out in the woods, cutting down trees and occasionally making some side money selling firewood from the bed of his truck. I learned that he had rolled his first GMC Denali pickup about a year earlier, and that he had bought his second Denali just before the shooting. As much as he loved the new truck, he was a little heartbroken about the demise of that first one, he said, because he had purchased it right after returning from Afghanistan. He bought it with the money he made as a military contractor for Blackwater.

He's been a merc, too? This guy's credentials include not just martial arts and the military, but also Blackwater? What is a jury going to think about that?

As my head spun with potential jury questions, Gerald went on reminiscing. He told me that he loved going to the coast, where he could take his sea kayak out on the water to catch cod and snapper. He spoke of diving for abalone near Brookings, a town on the Pacific at the Oregon-California border. Apparently this prized mollusk lives in waters as shallow as eight feet, but most of the trophy eleven-inchers can only be found at 25-feet deep or more. It takes a long, frigid free dive to harvest them, Gerald told me, in waters that are always dark and full of tidal currents. Sometimes sea lions sneaked up on him mid-dive, he said, scaring the hell out of him as they brushed by.

We talked like this for a long time, maybe 30 or 45 minutes. The two of us had a lot in common. Somewhere along the way I realized that I liked the guy, and I thought a jury would too, if it came to that. There was nothing in his manner or in the stories he told to back up the internet trolls' allegations of violent tendencies. But at this point, Gerald hadn't been charged with anything and I didn't know if he would be. It all depended on what the police thought happened on that roadway that night.

I went into the meeting without any intentions of asking Gerald to talk about the shooting. I consider it a big misstep, especially at a first meeting, to ask a client or would-be client who's accused of a crime to tell me their version of events. I like to let a little time pass for building trust and rapport before asking for the truth of what happened. But I will, indeed, ask a new client what they "think" they told the police and what evidence they "believe" the police have. That's important. Hearing the actual chain of events, however, should wait at least until after my client has had time to refresh his or her recollection by reviewing the police reports.

My experience is that clients will often tell me what they think *should* have happened, what they *wish* would have happened, or *what they think I want to hear*. They do this even though the truth is usually their best defense. Then, they get stuck in their story and don't want to admit that they lied to me – which creates big problems later on, when the evidence starts to conflict with their story.

I've seen this play out plenty of times. In one instance, a long-time client of mine confessed that his initial account of a crime was made up and that, actually, something else happened. I was elated when I learned that he had lied to me! His initial story would have made him the unluckiest guy in the world, putting him in the wrong place at the wrong time with the wrong stuff in his truck. When the truth came out it was clear that he did something that was morally wrong, no doubt, but not illegal.

Ideas about morality and protecting one's personal reputation … these can put good people in prison. The lies begin when somebody does something embarrassing but not criminal. Then their unwillingness to tell the truth lands them in court, facing criminal charges. I feared that any story Gerald might tell me could make him a victim of just that sort of scenario. Though I was afraid he might want to try, there really wasn't any way to stay looking good in society's eyes when it came to explaining how a motor vehicle collision escalated into a fatal shooting.

But clients trying to save face by telling lies is not all I worry about. Studies prove that human memory is faulty, especially during traumatic events in which our most basic fight-or-flight instinct takes control. From an evolutionary standpoint, remembering every detail about what happened in a life-or-death situation doesn't matter. Research shows that what we recall most clearly is the *outcome* of a situation. That's because it's the part that is most important for natural selection: you solved the problem and you lived on to procreate. Recalling the color of the stone tool you were carving when the lion started chasing you? That was not important to our ancestors, and it's still relatively unimportant today.

As soon as I finished providing Gerald with the legal information that I thought he needed to know, I found myself itching to break my initial-consult rule. I wanted him to tell me what happened. This wasn't an impulsive urge, I assured myself; it was based on the particular nature of this case and this potential client.

Time was of the essence. The case had not yet gone to grand jury. Whoever Gerald retained would have to act quickly to try to get this incident "no-filed" (not prosecuted). Police reports and evidence in the possession of law enforcement would be hard to come by unless a charge was lodged against him, meaning that whoever represented Gerald would have to work fast to create a narrative of the shooting that challenged the government's own. Knowing Gerald's side of the story would help me – if I got the job – figure out which experts to hire and which steps to take to flesh out his case.

If Gerald's story convinced me that it was indeed a case of self-defense, I'd continue to stand foursquare against having him talk to the police. Supreme Court Justice Robert H. Jackson famously wrote that "any lawyer worth his salt will tell the suspect in no uncertain terms to make no statement to the police under any circumstances." But I might take the unusual step of recommending that Gerald voluntarily testify at grand jury. In the hundreds of cases I had defended, I had never recommended that a client do this, but that's mostly because we're usually retained *after* someone is charged. In this case, it could save the guy years of his life and tens or hundreds of thousands of dollars in legal fees. Would I do it in Gerald's case? I couldn't know, not without hearing his version of events.

As I moved toward revealing some of my thinking to Gerald, I continued to internally question my motives. Was this just me seeking to satisfy my curiosity about how a professional fighter ended up shooting a man on a darkened roadway? Was I about to open a can of worms, legally speaking, that I'd live to regret? I'm not sure I was able to reason away either question satisfactorily, but I did have a strong and positive gut feeling about the man sitting across from me. If ever a client could handle the blunt question I wanted to ask, Gerald could. He was a Marine. He had been to Afghanistan. He lived a life of rigorous martial-arts discipline and had fought professionally before starting his own business. Beyond the obvious experience and wisdom gained from his career path, the man seemed honest. The self-deprecating stories he had told me showed that he was able to judge himself at arm's length, admit weaknesses and learn from his mistakes.

So, guided mainly by my sense that time was slipping away on any chance of getting the case no-filed, I did what I never do. I explained my rationale to him, and then took a deep breath and said, "Why don't you tell me what happened?"

He told me, and it was chilling.

"I'm on the way home with groceries so Kristin and I can make a nice dinner. There's a car in front of me. It slams on its brakes. I swerve around him to the right to avoid the collision. Before I can do anything he revs up and hits my truck. I'm in shock. He just hit my brand new truck. I can hear him yelling. He is threatening me. I can't start my truck. So I grab my gun and get out. I call 911. While I'm talking to the operator he keeps coming toward me. He sees my weapon. He says he's got a gun, too. I back up, telling him to stay away. But he keeps coming. He doesn't stop. I'm fearing for my life. So I pull the trigger. And he goes down. It was self-defense, Mike. Self-defense."

As Gerald spoke I watched his eyes, his mouth, his shoulders, and his hands. I realized that he was not just telling a story of what happened. He was re-living each moment, experiencing it all again. His face displayed anger, then fear, desperation, frustration … and at last, resolve. I could see that he was sweating, and I found myself identifying with him. I could imagine myself in precisely his place.

I believe him.

Not even my skeptical attorney's mind could convince me that this was anything but a justified, self-defense shoot. If ever there was a time when someone should have been entitled to kill a person, this scenario, out on the road, in the dark, facing a man who is threatening to kill you and says he is armed … well, this was it.

After a moment I said, quietly, "Gerald, that's unbelievable … but I believe it. That sounds justified."

Then I told him a little bit about how we try cases. I explained that "we prepare every case for settlement as if we were going to trial." We win by hard work and being prepared. I told him the bare-knuckled truth: this sort of aggressive defense would be expensive and time consuming. I suggested that he meet with some other lawyers both locally and in Portland, but Gerald was shaking his head before I could finish.

"I don't want to do that," Gerald said quietly but firmly. "I want to go with you."

"Look, Gerald, don't marry the first girl that says yes to a date. You've been married and divorced, right?"

"Yeah. Not too long ago."

"Choosing a lawyer is a more difficult and important decision than choosing a spouse. You choose your spouse poorly, and the consequences are a divorce that is messy and expensive. You choose a lawyer poorly, though, and you die in prison. Get it?"

He smiled wanly. "Yes, sir. I do."

"You need to completely and totally trust whoever you choose to represent you," I continued. "If you're indicted, you could be waiting for trial in the Lane County jail for a year or two. Your relationship with your attorney definitely will be challenged."

"I want to go with you," Gerald repeated. "I know what it's like to give someone all your trust. I trained to do that as a sniper. You and your spotter give each other 110 percent. If either one messes up, you die."

"True," I said, "but the difference between that relationship and ours is that if I mess up, you go to prison, and I go home to my family and a steak dinner, complaining about what a bad day I had at work."

"Mike, you ever hear of a Muay Thai fighter named Alex Gong?"

I hadn't. Gerald went on to tell how back in the summer of 2003 somebody did a hit-and-run on Alex's parked car. Alex saw it and gave chase on foot. When he caught up with the car and confronted the driver, the next thing he saw was a gun pointed in his face. "Alex died right there, on the street," Gerald told me. "Within minutes he went from doing his own thing on the street to being dead. Boom, gone. Dead in the street."

"What happened to the shooter?" I asked.

"Some dude they thought was the guy was confronted later by the cops and he killed himself."

"That's awful."

"I know. And I think maybe I was thinking of Alex the other night, in the back of my mind. Alex got killed because it didn't occur to him that he could get shot if he ran up on that car. I wasn't going to make that mistake. I wasn't going to let some random asshole kill me out there because I wasn't prepared."

What could I say to that? Nothing, so I sat there, and waited for him to continue.

"I've talked to Adam about you, and I've asked around," Gerald said, returning the conversation to the representation issue. "I'm sitting here in your office, looking you in the eyes. You believe me, don't you?"

"Yes."

"That's important to me. I need to retain an attorney who believes me, who believes *in* me."

"Sure, I do," I said. "But your defense needs more than that."

"Look, from where I'm sitting, you've got what I want in an attorney. I can tell just sitting here that you are the kind of guy who would fight, if he had to. You and me, we are the same like that; we're not too different actually. Since you played rugby, I know you can take a punch, probably a lot of them. Dish 'em out, too."

I chuckled. "I'm way better at taking punches, actually. That's more my skill set."

"But you're a fighter. I can tell. I don't think I'm going to find many men sitting on the other side of a desk that know what it's like to take a hit and bleed. You know what that's like."

I nodded.

Gerald continued, "I'm scared, Mike. I need someone who will fight as hard as I would. When I fight, I come out of my corner like my hair's on fire. I think you do, too. You have a plan and you sound eager to jump into this. I really like that. You've told me what you can do, and would do for me. Everything I've heard, I've liked. Plus, you haven't promised me anything, which tells me that you're realistic." For the first time in the meeting, he moved his body. He lifted his forearms and shoulders ever so slightly to indicate a shrug. "My mind is made up."

I stuck my hand out, and he grabbed it. We shook hands over my desk, and then I stood up and gave him one more out.

"You know, there isn't a big rush to make the decision. You can take a few days to interview other firms. I want you to be 100 percent sure that we're the right fit for you. I don't want you to regret your choice."

"Mike, I don't regret much. I can tell you right now, I won't regret this decision."

"Well, the real test will be whether or not you regret your decision a year from now. Or five years from now."

Gerald paused. Then he fixed his gaze on me and said, "Mike, I killed a man. He deserved to be shot but apparently he didn't need to be. That's the mistake I'll regret."

(Photo: Safeway surveillance video screenshot of Gerald minutes *before* the shooting)

(Photo: Springfield Police Department video screenshot of Gerald minutes *after* the shooting.)

Chapter 3: Getting to Work

Gerald signed the fee agreement that first day he walked into my office, January 31, 2014. That was a day that changed the course of my life, as surely as the night of January 29th had changed the course of Gerald's.

I had worked on many significant cases in my career, but none that had any real notoriety attached to it. My defendants were, at best, C-level characters in my D-level town. But this case was all over the news and my client was a local businessman with a network of customers and acquaintances. I knew that people would be asking questions of me, my attorneys and our staff, so I made sure to send out an office-wide email reminding all that the Strebendt case was just like any other case, and that we had duties of confidentiality to our client.

In the email I provided instructions about how to respond to people, but I didn't discourage anyone from discussing the case. On the contrary, I wanted to invite that discussion. I could tell already that this case needed to be thoroughly focus-grouped before going to trial. We needed as much insight as possible into our potential jurors, and I knew from experience that a lot of information could be gained even in casual conversations with friends and family – just so long as the conversations stuck to the facts that were known to the public.

I began work on the case the second Gerald walked out of my office. My initial goal, of course, was to prevent his case from ever going to a grand jury. If the district attorney did choose to take it to a grand jury, then the goal became avoiding an indictment. If he was indicted, my goal then was to turn over every stone of evidence and work toward dismissal or a plea agreement. And if all that failed, I would need to be ready for trial.

It was unusual to be starting work on a case this soon after an alleged crime. Normally, I wouldn't be retained until after the charge(s) had been filed, and I would come into the case knowing exactly what my client was alleged to have done. In this case, I could only speculate among all the possibilities: Murder, Manslaughter in the first degree ("Man I"), Man II, and Criminally Negligent Homicide. Murder was my biggest concern, of course. While Man I and Man II are very serious crimes, the length of the sentences pales when compared to what you face with Murder. There's a mandatory minimum sentence of ten years for Man I, 6 ¼ years for Man 2, and 25 to life for Murder. There was a lot at stake.

The first thing I would need to do in this case was figure out who I was going to have on my team. I would need support from an associate attorney, because I was already in deep water and struggling to swim with my current case load. I called Emilia within minutes of Gerald leaving the office.

She had to have seen that it was the office calling, because when she answered the phone, the first thing she said was, "No."

I laughed. "Aren't you at least interested in what I have to tell you?"

She didn't even hesitate. "Nope, not at all. Unless you intend to magic yourself to my house to clean up the entire box of Cheerios that Jacob just spilled on the floor, I'm not interested."

"The Springfield shooter came in today."

Now she was interested. "Really? Hey, did he tell you how to pronounce his last name? I've heard it about ten different ways in the last two days."

"*Stree*, rhymes with tree, and *bent*, like a piece of bent wire."

"*stree-BENT*." She sounded it out.

"No. *STREE-bent*. And he retained."

Now I'd gotten her full attention. "Wow, that's awesome, congrats! A murder case. How are you going to juggle it with your bazillion-count animal abuse case and your corporate case?"

"I thought you could bring in your littlest one, you know, to get some time off from managing two little guys at home. It could be a really good break for you, I think."

She didn't bite, but I'm not a quitter. Instead of pulling rank or coercing her, which I know from experience brings out her stubbornness and usually results in her doing the opposite of what I ask, I just started talking about the case. There were going to be a lot of moving parts to this defense, I told her – investigators, expert witnesses, psychologists, the list could get pretty long. Then, before she could interrupt me, I told her about my meeting with Gerald – how he looked and sounded when he told me what had happened on the Bob Straub Parkway that night. And I told her that I believed him.

When I finished, there was silence for a moment. Then Emilia ended the call by rather half-heartedly telling me that she'd "think about participating" in Gerald's defense. But, not long after we hung up, she texted me: "Did you find out if Karlin is available to work this case? He needs to get down here now." *Got her*, I thought.

Knowing that Emilia would be in the office soon enough, I started to lay out the building blocks of the case. I was in what I call the "golden hour," the first hour after a client retains me. It's a time when there are no documents to review yet, and no reports or statements crowding my mind and entrenching my beliefs about the case. Like walking into my office with the accused for the first time and viewing him as a juror would, it's another really important time when I can play the role of a fact-finder who is hearing the details of the case for the first time. If I'm going to have creative ideas about my defense strategy, they'll probably come to the fore in these first 60 minutes.

As much as I'd believed Gerald's story, I knew I wouldn't be doing him any favors by simply accepting it as he told it. I needed to *establish* the truth of his account, and yes, Emilia was right; I'd have to start by getting a forensic accident reconstructionist out to the scene. My first choice was David Karlin of the Portland based Talbott and Associates. I needed this MIT-trained engineer to drop everything, take a look at the scene, and then try to reconstruct the accident that triggered the shooting.

First and foremost, I wanted to know if the evidence supported what Gerald said happened and when. If Karlin's results showed me I could trust Gerald's account, I could build the entire framework for his defense on that trust. Second, I wanted Karlin's report to tell me what the government likely already knew. I wouldn't be able to access any police reports until the charges got filed, which to me was too late. If we wanted to avoid charges, it was imperative that we get up to speed on the government's view of the case and fast.

Karlin agreed to drive down and meet with me. After I apologized for asking him to drop everything, he replied, "Come on, Mike, this is what we do. Besides, in case you didn't know, it rains in Oregon and that's no good for evidence. I will see you tomorrow at the latest."

That was an understatement. We have two seasons in Eugene: summer and the rainy season. Being it was January, it had rained off and on since Gerald had shot the man now identified as David Crofut. Skid marks, slide marks, bits of fabric, even the paint chips found after a collision provide clues about speed, force, and directionality in a car vs. car collision, but precipitation degrades them pretty quickly. Still, I knew that if there was evidence to find, Karlin would find it.

I met Karlin in 2009 during another death case. That one was a civil products liability suit filed against a motorcycle helmet manufacturer/distributor. My client's wife was killed after her helmet came off of her head during a car vs. motorcycle collision. Karlin established himself as the meticulous, articulate, and egghead-ish expert that I like to have explaining physics to jurors. With his glasses and accountant's manner, he looks and acts like somebody you ought to pay attention to, yet behind the scenes, his offbeat personality makes him fun to work with. I like to say that if anyone needs to attend sensitivity training, it's Karlin. He's continually cracking jokes that are so incredibly inappropriate, always delivered with such a straight face – well, you can't help but bust up laughing even in the most tragic and gruesome circumstances. I can't count the number of times he left my entire team in stitches, just from hearing some quietly outrageous comment across the walkie-talkies.

But I also respect Karlin as a military veteran who enlisted at the age of 18 – with the Israeli Defense Forces, that is. He's seen a lot, he tells it straight, and when it comes to an investigation, his opinion is not for sale. He's told me that my theory of a case was wrong far more often than he's told me I'm right.

The next call I made was to Verne Hoyer, an investigator I'd used many times before. Verne was forced to retire from a patrol job with the Eugene Police Department when a freak wood-splitting accident blinded him in one eye. Verne's son was doing the splitting when a shard of metal broke off a cheap, Chinese-made molded steel maul and flew 20 feet to strike his dad in the eye.

Verne is a story-teller, and it's almost impossible to get him out of the office when he's on a roll. He has two claims to fame in law enforcement: he was a first responder to the University of Oregon's football stadium murder/suicide shooting in 1984 and he was involved in the apprehension of the I-5 Killer, a notorious serial murder case.

I met Verne a few years earlier when we worked together on a self-defense case in Depoe Bay, Oregon, a picturesque coastal town that claims to have the smallest natural navigable sea harbor in the world. My client, Mark Dade, was vacationing at the coast with relatives when he was accused of punching the very elderly Vietnamese owner of a local Shell gas station. Mark is a big man, and the little, wrinkled gas station owner was anything but.

The case was a great lesson in "looks may be deceiving," exemplifying how confirmation bias can totally destroy the legitimacy of an investigation. Confirmation bias is when law enforcement (or anybody) has their mind made up about an individual or a situation before hearing all the facts. It's about filtering everything you see or hear through a lens colored by your own beliefs. Psychological research shows that the only way to avoid confirmation bias is to acknowledge that you may have been influenced to a conclusion without having the facts to back it up. Then you have to actively function as your own devil's advocate, seeking out opposing evidence and viewpoints.

The local police couldn't do that in the gas station case, but Verne could. He was able to confirm what Mark and his family had told me from the beginning: that Mark had only punched the gas station owner after the little Vietnamese man had physically attacked his elderly grandfather – Mark's father, really, who had raised Mark since babyhood, when his birth parents were the victims of a double homicide. Police may have assumed that the tragic loss of his birth parents predisposed Mark to violent acts. Witnesses to the gas station incident may have assumed Mark's guilt because they saw only the part where a big white guy threw a punch at a wizened old immigrant defending his property. But, via his investigation, Verne established that this "little old man" was well-known for freaking out if a tourist used the station restroom without buying gas. Verne was able to track down witnesses to prior instances of the owner's anger, and to impeach several of the prosecution's witnesses when they changed their stories at trial. Presumably their stories changed to try to help the perceived victim, underscoring the importance of truth-seeking – without bias – in any investigation.

Now I needed Verne Hoyer's investigative skills to start locating witnesses to anything and everything that happened the night of January 29, 2014. Only two days had gone by, yet I knew that memories were fading and shifting even as I sat at my desk making phone calls. We needed to have had people located and interviewed yesterday. The longer it took us to find them, the less detail they would recall, and the less trustworthy their recollection would be. Things change. People relocate, change their job or their name, join the military, and even die before you can get a case to verdict. Just as I needed Karlin ASAP, I had to get Verne on the job immediately.

It wasn't more than three hours later that I received by phone the first bit of evidence from Verne.

"Mike, I have some news," he said. "I got a tip where Crofut was coming from before the collision – the Driftwood Pub. I talked to several witnesses there, including two bartenders who served both him and his wife, Brenda." Verne said he had also talked to the bar's owner. "He looked at the receipts and did the math, and confirmed that David Crofut may have consumed between six and eight Pyramid Hefeweizen beers immediately before the accident."

I began googling the alcohol content of a Pyramid Hef. "Were they 12, 16 or 22-ounce beers?" I asked. My previous experience in both prosecuting and defending hundreds of driving under the influence of intoxicant (DUII) cases was about to come in handy, I thought.

"16-ounce pints," Verne replied.

"Damn!" I exclaimed. "Somebody was drunk and had a motive to hit and run – to avoid a drunk-driving charge. That doesn't get us to self-defense but it might start explaining this guy's behavior. What do you want to bet he's a regular there?"

"He was starting to be a regular," Verne explained. "He and Brenda had recently moved down from the Tacoma area after he sold his tavern up there."

"What do you bet he wakes up in the morning at a .02 fairly regularly?" I asked, not really expecting an answer. I know this guy's type and his patterns from the DUIIs.

"One patron said that he had offered the Crofuts a ride home that night, worried that they'd had too much to drink," he told me. "They declined."

"Worst decision of their lives," I said.

"I'll call you back when I have more," Verne assured me. "I have a feeling there's more to the story at the bar."

With that information in my pocket, I called Springfield Detective Rick Lewis, who had been commenting to the press pretty consistently and appeared to be the lead detective on the case. The day after the shooting, Lewis was quoted as saying, "[The case] remains open and uncharged at this point because there's been a claim of self-defense."

I needed to get Karlin in to see the vehicles and I hoped that by contacting Lewis I could make that happen. I was also curious about what Lewis would be willing to tell me about the case once I told him that Gerald had hired our office to represent him.

Just by being a consumer of local TV news, I had noticed that Lewis got in front of the camera a lot more than I was accustomed to seeing from a police detective. He was a guy in his fifties with close-cropped hair, somebody who had obviously spent a lot of time in the gym getting big. He came off confident, well-spoken and fairly friendly, as most successful and well-liked officers do.

After introducing myself to Lewis, I asked, "Do you know who's in charge of the case for the District Attorney's Office?"

"Bob Lane's handling it," he told me.

"Is it being grand juried?" I asked, hoping to milk some information out of him regarding the likelihood of Gerald getting charged with something. Knowledge is power at this stage of the game and the police had a lot more of both than I did.

"You'll have to talk to Bob about that," he replied. "Do you think there's any way we could sit down and talk with Mr. Strebendt about his self-defense claim?"

"I doubt it but I can check," I told him.

After concluding the conversation with Lewis, I called the D.A.'s office. I talked to Bob Lane, the lead prosecutor on Lane County's Major Crimes Team – and found, to no surprise, that he was playing his cards closer than Lewis was. I could tell I wouldn't be seeing him on the TV news anytime soon.

Lane had never been fond of giving interviews to the press. In fact, he sometimes refused to speak about cases to anybody. In a county where there are only 28 district attorneys and hardly more than 23 practicing trial lawyers in the entire office, everybody knows everybody by record and personality type. On the job, Lane is known as a just-the-facts-ma'am kind of prosecutor, not much concerned with winning the affections of jurors. Off the job, he's the kind of guy who has earned his stripes as an introvert, choosing to work in his garden or fish with older colleagues in his spare time. Outside of his circle of friends, he's a man of few words. In fact, there's a story told of an eager young D.A. who walked into the break room once to find Lane reading a newspaper. The youngster tried to strike up a conversation, but Lane wasn't having any. Lane slowly moved the newspaper down from his face to size up the whippersnapper in front of him … and then, without uttering a sound, slowly moved the paper back up and continued reading.

With a legal pad rapidly filling with notes from these phone calls, I now had the beginnings of a trial outline. It's in part a to-do list and in part a script for trial. I'm a big believer in thinking about my opening statement, jury selection and even my closing argument, right from Day One. I encourage my associates to do the same. In my characteristic scrawl I saw a shopping list of experts to hire:

- *Firearms and ballistics*

- *Physical evidence (gun powder residue, blood/blood spatter, hair, clothes)*

- *GMC Denali (someone who knows the particulars of Gerald's truck)*

- *Psychologist (PTSD testing)*

Pondering the situation further, I added three more to-do's, all three of them very important to accomplish ASAP:

- *Establish website (to let people find us if they have information)*

- *Develop Media Plan (for getting out Gerald's side of the story)*

- *Call Peter Jarvis (our firm's ethics counsel in Portland)*

Gerald was getting slain in local and national media, even at this early stage of the case. That very morning Oregon's largest newspaper, *The Oregonian*, reported the titillating details in their headline "Minor Car Accident in Springfield Involving Former

Sniper Leads to Fatal Shooting." The first paragraph identified Gerald Strebendt as a professional mixed martial artist who allegedly "gunned down" David Crofut. This article created the impression that the collision was no big deal and that this man who had the ability to defend himself with his hands used a gun to execute someone outside of the safety of a vehicle. Here was Oregon's leading media source, claiming that my client "gunned down" an unarmed man. This I would not tolerate.

KEZI-TV (Eugene's ABC affiliate) was a little more accurate, calling the collision a "crash" rather than a "minor accident." Words and descriptions matter. They have long-lasting effects on the minds of potential jurors that reporters fail to consider when they write stories. During the same TV report, Springfield Detective Lewis hinted at a motive, saying that the shooting had something to do with driving behavior before the collision, but that they were interested in learning more through their investigation. It was disappointing to see a seasoned detective portraying a purported theory of motive as fact.

These were just a few examples of the ways my jury pool had already been salted with negative, even false, publicity about what happened on that road that night. I knew from reading the psychological research that negative publicity on a client or a case causes confirmation bias and source confusion to set in very rapidly. It's crucial to get accurate, unbiased information out there as quickly as possible to level the playing field.

With this in mind, I wanted to discuss with our firm's ethics lawyer, Peter Jarvis, what I could do for Gerald in the media within the confines of the Oregon Rules of Professional Responsibility. Most lawyers with ethics questions call the free Oregon State Bar number to get advice. There you can get information on a variety of issues, including pre-trial publicity ethics, but in my experience, you get what you pay for. I prefer to call an expert and be done with it, and Jarvis is the best ethics lawyer in the Northwest. I'd rather pay him and know I'm getting a fast, accurate reading of what I can and can't do than to rely on government-paid bar advisors who may try hard but have no personal malpractice risk of their own to better incentivize them to get it right.

I wasn't a newbie here; Gerald's situation wasn't our first media case. In fact, I had one case that really galvanized my belief that the defense owes its clients every effort that is ethical to get its side of the story before the public.

Several years earlier, we defended a hit-and-run charge where our client may have acted in self-defense. Driving his Dodge pickup truck, he ran down and nearly killed a Mongol outlaw motorcycle gang member. Immediately after the incident he fled in fear for his life. He was terrified to turn himself in because he knew that the victim was a confidential police informant who perhaps worked with the same detectives that were investigating the attempted murder charge stemming from the hit-and-run. My client was also afraid to be tried or incarcerated locally, because he thought the victim had gang connections in jail.

Since my client was thought to have left the state, there was a fugitive warrant out for him. On my client's behalf I bypassed local authorities and instead contacted the U.S. Marshals, agreeing to turn in my client at the federal courthouse in downtown Eugene. When interviewed by local reporter Jack Moran about it, I said that the victim had threatened my client with violence and claimed an affiliation with the Mongols motorcycle club. The reporter then confirmed through the Mongols that the victim was indeed a former member of the biker club. The victim later showed me a large Mongols tattoo on his neck, proof of his background, and confirmed his role as an informant.

I can write about this case because it's now a matter of public record – I *made* it part of the public record by talking to the press with my client's permission. It was part of my larger Media Plan for that case. However, it instantly angered the district attorney on the case, who apparently believes that press contact is exclusively the domain of the police. There was talk of an ethics complaint against me, but it never materialized – probably an idea that was dropped after the office conducted a group reading of the ethics rule on pretrial publicity and learned how off-base they were in criticizing me. But it didn't stop the assigned D.A. from allegedly telling a colleague that my office was "walking the line, ethically speaking."

I would like to clarify that there is no "walking the line." There is no cloudy middle ground that gradually pulls you to the dark side of the bar when you approach it. It is no different than walking down a sidewalk. Technically, you are always walking the line, and you could stray into traffic and be killed instantly. But it's silly to worry about that. Just keep moving forward.

So, I say to hell with the holier-than-thou misconception among prosecutors and even some defense attorneys that a lawyer should never talk to the press. Are we to believe that the media can only be used by the government for "perp walks" or leaks of negative information from police public information officers? No, absolutely not. Aware of the psychological research on confirmation bias and source confusion, I long ago came to the conclusion that it is essentially malpractice to avoid the press when you have an innocent client. There are enough obstacles in the way of defending a client against the weight of the government. Self-imposed limitations on the use of the press should not add to the burden.

Going further, I'd say that our legal process only works fairly so long as both sides are playing the same game and having an equal opportunity to speak publicly. If only the government is playing the press game of checkers and the defense refuses to participate, the government is always going to win. Consequently, you will never, ever find me saying "no comment" when a reporter calls. It's my duty to make a move and at least use the opportunity to educate the public about the jury system and the presumption of innocence.

Later on that afternoon, I decided to add yet one more item to my growing list...

The Rest of *Finishing Machine* is available on Amazon.com.

About the Authors

Mike Arnold is a trial attorney in Eugene, Oregon. He grew up in Parkville, Missouri, and moved to Oregon to attend law school. He tells stories for a living, delivering a narrative through facts and evidence to juries around the state. Often, these courtroom stories end with a **jury's two-word verdict**. Mike also enjoys telling stories to his daughter. These tend to be more complicated tales that reveal, to Abigail's dismay, that someone in the family is actually an alien or a robot.

Mike gained notoriety as an attorney when he stood on the courthouse steps as **Ammon Bundy's attorney** and told the remaining occupiers of the Malheur Wildlife Refuge to "please stand down." In the aftermath of the standoff he was credited with assisting in the negotiation of a **peaceful resolution** for the four remaining holdouts of the Oregon occupation.

Another of Mike's murder cases was featured on a **CBS "48 Hours" episode** entitled "Trail of Tears."

Mike is also the host of a legal podcast called "**Law Is War with Mike Arnold**," which includes **episodes** with analysis of the **Ammon Bundy** (Oregon Standoff) verdict, murder of **Nancy Cooper**, trial **objections**, **jury selection**, **jury nullification**, etc.

Emilia Gardner is an Oregon attorney. Reading was her first love, and there were no bounds to what genre of book she could and would curl up with and enjoy. A love of writing soon followed, but it would never take the place of consuming the words on the page written by others. Emilia is a straightforward woman and attorney, and her communication style is evident in her writing: simple, to the point, and effective.

(Photo: The authors celebrating after winning bail for a
client in murder case in Hood River, Oregon.)

VersusPublishing.com - MikeArnold.com